3·75

SPECIAL
SERMONS
ON THE FAMILY

SPECIAL
SERMONS
ON THE FAMILY

by

GEORGE SWEETING

MOODY PRESS
CHICAGO

Library of Congress Cataloging in Publication Data

Sweeting, George, 1924—
    Special sermons on the family.

    1. Family—Religious life—Sermons.
2. Sermons, American. I. Title.
BV4526.2.S768   248.4   81-873
ISBN 0-8024-8208-2   AACR2

Printed in the United States of America

With warm appreciation to
Herman Braunlin
E. Brandt Gustavson
James A. Gwinn
Donald E. Hescott
Lawrence E. Pearson

Special gratitude is extended to
Phil Johnson, who has assisted
me in research and editing.

Contents

1

The Dangers of an Unequal Yoke

Divorce in America is reaching epidemic proportions. Almost half of the marriages begun each year end in divorce before the fifth anniversary. In the high population areas of our nation the number of divorces granted annually exceeds the number of marriages performed. And the statistics on divorce are growing worse.

A common excuse for divorce is incompatibility— inability to meet the needs and expectations of the partner. Marriage is bonding, a uniting of two different persons; and compatibility is vital for harmony in the union. But a biblical marriage requires more than just physical or emotional compatibility. Spiritual compatibility is also required, because marriage is a spiritual union as well as a physical, mental, and emotional one. And it is my conviction that the sense of incompatibility that is often felt between marriage partners is at its root *spiritual* incompatibility—the inability to have oneness of mind in spiritual matters.

Of course, spiritual incompatibility is likely when two unbelievers marry, because without faith in the authority of the Word of God, there is no basis for spiritual unity. But when a believer marries an unbeliever, spiritual incompatibility is inevitable.

There seem to be few things as clear in Scripture as the teaching that a believer should not marry an unbeliever. But despite the clarity of God's Word and the evidence from actual experience that such marriages involve risk, marriages between Christians and non-Christians occur today with greater frequency than ever. And the divorce rate for such couples continues to rise at a staggering rate; divorce between couples of differing faiths occurs three times as often as divorce between members of the same faith.

The thrill of loving and of being loved temporarily minimizes all obstacles to a mixed marriage. The excitement of the wedding plans, the beauty of the ceremony, and all that goes with marriage and the anticipation of a new life temporarily carries the young couple along on the assumption that all will be well because their love is so deep it can conquer any problem. But reality soon manifests itself, and the problems of what God's Word calls an unequal yoke cannot be pushed aside.

The effects of a marriage between a Christian and a non-Christian are many and far-reaching. What are some of those effects? I would like to examine them from three perspectives.

The Upward Effects

First, let us look at *the upward effects*. How does marrying an unbeliever affect a Christian's relationship with God?

One of the obvious effects of a mixed marriage is carelessness about the things of God. That is understandable! The believer often drops his church connections and grows increasingly indifferent, silently at first, but more openly as time passes. What causes such a decline?

Remember that, at its root, a believer's marriage to an unbeliever is defiance of God and His order. The clear command of God is that a believer should not be "unequally yoked together with unbelievers" (2 Corinthians 6:14), and marriage to an unbeliever is an example of such an unequal yoke. A marriage that begins in rebellion to God can hardly expect His blessing.

Olivia Langedon was a believer. But she was in love with a young author, Samuel Clemens (whom we know as Mark Twain), and he was not a believer. In fact he was a skeptic. But she felt that her love for him was great enough to overcome any obstacles, and besides, she was a good influence on him. So she married him.

At first it seemed to be working, but as the years went by he showed more and more antagonism to her beliefs. One day as she was reading the Bible aloud, he strongly protested, "I don't believe the Bible. I can't sit here and listen to it."

Not only was there no unity of faith between them, but his unbelief produced a paralyzing effect on her until her faith was destroyed as well! After many years, while they were passing through days of sorrow, Mark Twain tried to comfort his wife. "Olivia, if it comforts you to lean on the Christian faith, do so."

"I can't," she said. "I haven't any left."

A mixed marriage can mean loss of faith as well as loss of fellowship with the heavenly Father. When we behave contrary to His direction we forfeit the possibility of a close walk with the Lord.

Not only that, but God is not glorified in a mixed marriage. Marriage is presented in the Bible as a sort of divine object lesson—a picture of the relationship of Christ and the church. Marriage of a believer to an unbeliever corrupts the purity of that lesson. Christ's union with the church is perfect, flawless. A marriage between two believers pictures that unity, with the potential of perfect spiritual, emotional, and physical unity. But a marriage involving a believer and an unbeliever cannot illustrate perfect unity, and so it cannot bring glory to God.

Second, what are some of *the inward effects* of mixed marriages? What is the effect on a believer when he chooses to unite in marriage with an unbeliever?

A lady who asked to speak to me concerning marriage was deeply moved as she related her story. "Before our marriage John attended church with me and showed signs of spiritual interest. He promised to make a spiritual decision after our marriage, but he never has. During our eight years of marriage he has never attended church. He shows nothing but bitterness toward anything spiritual in the home. My children are not being trained. Our home is not a reflection of heaven. My heart is broken. If only I had obeyed the Scriptures!"

Not long ago a man came to my office to tell me of his broken marriage. "Why didn't someone warn me of those things?" he said. "I never dreamed we'd have so many differences."

And aside from the heartache and bitterness that can grow out of a mixed marriage, there are some very serious spiritual consequences for the believer who marries an unbeliever. Those consequences are inescapable for several reasons.

One of the primary reasons is that the marriage of a true believer and an unbeliever lacks common ground of purpose. Amos wrote, "Can two walk together, except they be agreed?" (Amos 3:3).

Because the unbeliever will not rise to a life of faith, the believer must bow to a life of unbelief. On the Lord's day one wants to worship with the Lord's people while the other wants to sleep. The believer wants to give to God's work, and the unbeliever maintains that they cannot afford to do so. Sunday is a holy day to the believer but a holiday to the unbeliever. Times of crisis come, and they are not able to pray together. The unbeliever may even despise the convictions of the believer and ridicule his faith.

All of that can put a strain on the spiritual activities of the believer and therefore weaken his relationship with the Lord. He begins to neglect God's Word, because spending time in the Word is frowned on by the unbelieving mate.

Guilt feelings can build and grow, both from the guilt of marrying out of God's will and from the guilt of neglected spiritual responsibilities. The believer's prayer life is adversely affected. He may become severely depressed, as many have who have married out of the Lord's will. Or he may become resentful of the Lord or of other Christians and in the end forsake fellowship with other believers altogether.

The Outward Effects

Finally, what are *the outward effects* of a mixed marriage? What effect on a believer's spouse, his children, his family, his in-laws, and those around him can result from marriage to an unbeliever?

The Bible speaks of a few people who willfully disobeyed their parents in choosing a life partner. Esau, it seems, delighted in disobeying his parents. According to Genesis 28:8, Esau saw "that the daughters of Canaan pleased not Isaac his father," yet he had deliberately chosen a wife from among them. He treated his parents' wishes with contempt, and the whole family and his offspring for generations paid bitterly for his sin.

Samson likewise flouted the counsel of his parents, and as a result his entire family was engulfed in sorrow. The curse of God falls upon those who have no concern for parental guidance, and the effects of their sin touch everyone around them.

For the believer blessed with a believing mother and father, a mixed marriage is only a source of sorrow both to himself and to his parents. The unbelieving mate frequently destroys all the fruit of the believing parents' loving labor in the spiritual growth of their child, and it can hardly be expected that they will respond favorably to the unbelieving son- or daughter-in-law. That results in a strain of the family relations, which is a source of grief in itself.

Children are the biggest losers in mixed marriages. Any church affiliation they might have is usually superficial. Because of the lack of agreement in principles between the parents, discipline tends to be inconsistent, and the child can become confused. There is no unity of conviction, and thus there is continual conflict.

In the law of Moses, the children of Israel were forbidden to yoke the ox and the ass together. Why? The ox and the ass were very different in size, strength, and temperament. To yoke them together was not only unfitting but unfair as well. Both suffered discomfort from the unequal yoking, and they could not work well together. It is possible that that is what Paul had in mind when he wrote to the Corinthians urging them to stop being yoked together with unbelievers. For a believer to be yoked in marriage to an unbeliever is cruel. Marriage between a believer and an unbeliever is a poor working relationship and a source of injury and anguish to both partners.

God forbade the Israelites to marry outsiders, "for they will turn away thy son from following me that they may serve other gods," (Deuteronomy 7:4). Marrying an unbeliever is the same as marrying his unbelief.

Soft words and mellow phrases are often used to make it sound better, but the truth is that people who do not think the same on vital spiritual issues have no business getting married! They cannot be together for long without both becoming very unhappy.

It is generally true that if a young man or young woman will not receive Christ before the wedding, he or she will not do so after the honeymoon is over.

18

The time to deal with the question of marrying an unbeliever is before becoming involved with one. If you are single, perhaps you should purpose, as many dedicated Christians have, not to date anyone who is not spiritually compatible with you.

The wife of Matthew Henry, the renowned Bible commentator, was the only daughter of a wealthy merchant. When Matthew Henry sought permission to marry her, her father refused. He said that while Matthew was polite, scholarly, and nice, he was a stranger to the family. "Why, I don't even know where he comes from," insisted the father.

"True," replied the daughter, "but I know where he is going and would like to go with him."

Apparently her father saw the point and granted his permission for the marriage. She had her priorities straight. She understood that spiritual compatibility was far more important than any other requirement for a prospective mate. When two people truly love the Lord with all their hearts and love each other, God's blessing will go with them.

Make sure that the life partner you choose is a believer who sincerely wants the will of God. Make Christ the center of your wedding plans. Determine to do His will, to be obedient to Him, and to build your family around Him.

"But," you may be saying, "the problems you have mentioned describe our home exactly. My mate is not a believer. I have disobeyed God. My spiritual fervor is diminished. I am a defeated Christian because of it, and I would give anything if I could undo the damage I have done. Is there hope for me?"

Yes, thank God, there is always hope. God has promised to forgive our sin if we confess it. We may still have to live with some of the consequences of our sin, but we do not have to be defeated.

Purpose to yield your life more completely to God.

Determine to love your mate more than ever and pray regularly for his or her conversion. God will multiply His grace to you if you truly seek His best for you and submit fully to His will.

2

Wanted: Christian Parents

Several years ago an eminent sociologist and author made an amazing prediction. The day might come, he said, when parents would let experts raise their children. We would see newspaper advertisements like this:

Why let parenthood tie you down? Let us raise your infant into a responsible, successful adult. Class A Pro-family offers: father age 30, mother, 36, grandmother, 67. Uncle and aunt, age 30, live in, hold part-time local employment. Four-child-unit has opening for one, age 6-8. Regulated diet exceeds government standards. All adults certified in child development and management. Bio-parents permitted frequent visits. Telephone contact allowed. Child may spend summer vacation with bio-parents. Religion, art, music encouraged by special arrangement. Five year contract, minimum. Write for further details.

That prediction, by the way, was made by Dr. Alvin Toffler in his best-selling book *Future Shock*.[1] Another prominent author, Ferdinand Lundberg, in *The Coming World Transformation* made a similar prediction. He claims that the family as we know it is near the point of extinction.[2]

And there is some troubling evidence that in the past few decades there has been a serious decline in the traditional family. The divorce rate is soaring, homosexuality is touted as an alternate life-style, and in a large number of American

21

families, because both the mother and the father work, the children are left at home alone to run the house.

Of course, Bible-believing Christians deplore those developments. We believe that God's standards for the family are absolute and that the family is essential to the survival of our nation. In fact, the very turbulence of the times in which we live makes the ties of home and family more important than ever. And although writers and commentators are boldly saying that conventional marriage has seen its day, and although permissive sex abounds, the marriage commitment and a stable home life remain first choice for the great majority of young people.

Better than anyone else, you that are parents know why that is true. Although it costs a great deal to establish and carry on a home, no other pattern of life can provide so much love and joy and genuine satisfaction. God has made the family an institution whose foundations are love, satisfaction, and mutual service. And when that institution passes away, it will mark the end of our existence as a people.

Why did God establish the family? Why is the family unit so crucial? Why could not the same love be shared in a different environment? What is it about the conventional family that God uses? I am persuaded that God designed the family for several reasons, but one of the primary reasons is the challenging task of caring for, nurturing, and training children—a task that could not be adequately fulfilled by any other means than the conventional family.

No other calling is more crucial. Great men in places of leadership make far-reaching decisions in government, science, and business. But parents set the course of a whole new generation! What an opportunity! And what a responsibility!

Each child is eternally important. That little human life God gave you at the birth of that tiny child will continue on, in heaven or in hell, forever. In his brief life on this earth he will leave a trail of blessing or a trail of ruin. And before he leaves this globe, he in turn will play a part in shaping the generation still to come.

The calling of a mother or father is the most important calling on earth. If you are a parent, your responsibility to your children is more important than your job, your hobbies, or anything else you could spend your life on. And parenting never has been a greater challenge than right now. The storms that lash and batter the family today have never been more violent. You ask, What can we do? Is there any hope? How can we fortify our homes? Can we prepare our children for what is ahead?

Yes, God's Word does give us some guidelines. In fact, if we go as far back as the Old Testament book of Deuteronomy, we find that even when God gave Moses the law, He had a word for the parents. Listen to the Word of God from Deuteronomy 6:5-9:

> And thou shalt love the LORD thy God with all thine heart, and with all thy soul, and with all thy might.
>
> And these words, which I command thee this day, shall be in thine heart:
>
> And thou shalt teach them diligently unto thy children, and thou shalt talk of them when thou sittest in thine house, and when thou walkest by the way, and when thou liest down, and when thou risest up.
>
> And thou shalt bind them for a sign upon thine hand, and they shall be as frontlets between thine eyes.
>
> And thou shalt write them upon the posts of thy house, and on thy gates.

In that passage, I see three guidelines for parenting, and they all deal with the Word of God.

LOVE THE WORD

First, to be successful parents, we are told, we must *love the Word of God.* Love for God includes love for His Word. "Love the Lord thy God," it says, "and these words . . . shall be in thine heart." You cannot love God unless you love His Word, and you cannot love God's Word unless you truly love Him.

Centuries later than Moses, Jesus said that this is the most important commandment in all the Bible, and it certainly is the foundation on which we must build our families.

Notice that we are to love God with all our heart, soul, and mind. "Your heart" means your spirit—that part of you that is able to worship and have a relationship with God. "Your soul" includes the rest of your immaterial being—your mind, emotions, and will. And "your might" refers to your physical being, or your body. What this verse is saying is that our love for God and for His Word must consume every part of our being—body, soul, and spirit.

Love results in obedience. Jesus said, "If a man love me, he will keep my words . . . He that loveth me not keepeth not my sayings" (John 14:23-24). The greatest thing you as a parent can give to your children is an example of loving obedience to God and to His Word.

Paul wrote to Timothy of the faith that had been in his grandmother, Lois, and in his mother, Eunice (2 Timothy 1:5). In the same epistle Paul reminded Timothy "that from a child thou hast known the holy Scriptures, which are able to make thee wise unto salvation through faith which is in Christ Jesus" (2 Timothy 3:15). Timothy had a grandmother and a mother who loved the Word of God, and Paul was reminding him that that was the greatest heritage he had. Timothy went on to become one of the greatest leaders in the early church.

TEACH THE WORD

But it is not enough just to love the Word of God. David

loved the Word of God, but that did not make him a good parent. We must also *teach the Word of God.* We cannot expect our children to find the right way by themselves. God's Word reveals the way to salvation, security, and satisfaction, but each generation must be shown. They must be taught the Word of God.

Deuteronomy 6:7 says, "Thou shalt teach them diligently unto thy children." As parents it is not enough just to love and honor God ourselves. We must also teach our children, both with our lives and with our lips.

You cannot begin to teach your children too soon or repeat your teaching too often. The command is to speak about God's Word "when thou sittest in thine house, and when thou walkest by the way, and when thou liest down, and when thou risest up." God is saying to teach your children in every situation of life—morning, noon, and night. When you are at home, when you are driving in your car, while picnicking in the park, when you tuck them in at night, when they get up in the morning, teach them! Teach them!

Teach your children that God is the Creator, that He loves them, that He answers prayer. Teach them that wrong is wrong and right is right, and that sin destroys and separates. Teach them that we reap what we sow, and that the wages of sin is death. Teach them that Christ died for their sins according to the Scriptures and that He was buried, and that He rose again the third day. Teach them that whosoever believeth in Him should not perish but have everlasting life. Teach them diligently.

At least five times in slightly different ways the Bible says that the fear of the Lord is the beginning of wisdom. What a powerful phrase! The child in your home may become a brilliant scholar, he may receive degrees and honor and fame. But if he does not learn to know and honor God and His Word, he will grope and tumble and stumble through life as a failure and as a fool.

Only God's Word applied to the life has the power to cleanse and deliver and give light. In Psalm 119:9, the psalmist asks, "Wherewithal shall a young man cleanse his way?" And then he answers, "By taking heed thereto according to thy word." Teach your children *how* to apply the Word to their lives.

Happy is the young man or young woman whose parents have taught him to allow the Word of God to correct and shape his life. Long after that father and mother have stepped aside, the Bible will reprove him and guide him.

Paul wrote to Timothy and reminded him that he had known the Word of God from his childhood. Then he made this poignant observation: "All scripture is given by inspiration of God, and is profitable for doctrine, for reproof, for correction, for instruction in righteousness" (2 Timothy 3:16). That means that the ministry of the Word of God in a person's life is a ministry of discipline.

What is discipline? My dictionary defines it as "training that corrects, molds, or perfects the mental faculties or moral character." Discipline, my friend, involves shaping and correction. It takes place only when the person involved can subject himself to another's authority. Hebrews 12:5-6 says, "My son, despise not thou the chastening of the Lord, nor faint when thou art rebuked of him: For whom the Lord loveth he chasteneth, and scourgeth every son whom he receiveth."

Parent, are you teaching your children that they cannot expect to call all the signals in their lives? Can they accept authority? They will have to learn eventually, but so many learn too late!

And are you teaching your children that they must be saved from their sin? By far your greatest responsibility as a parent to your child is to lead him to personal faith in Christ as his Savior. Do not assume that because he has gone to Sunday school and church, to summer camp or Bible club,

26

to vacation Bible school or to a local Christian school, that he has personally accepted Christ as his own. You cannot afford to be afraid or ashamed to talk to him personally about it.

<h2 align="center">KEEP THE WORD</h2>

Finally, Deuteronomy 6:8-9 says that it is our responsibility as parents to *keep the Word of God.* We are to bind the Word on our hands, put it as a frontlet between our eyes, and put it at the entrance to our houses. Traditional Jews bind their arms and foreheads with phylacteries when they pray, and put mezuzahs on doorposts because of this verse. But I am convinced that the meaning of the verse goes far deeper than that.

Binding the Word on our arms signifies the *practice* of God's Word. Deuteronomy 6:8 is saying that whatever our hands do, they should be guided by the Word of God. The Bible gives us direction as Christian parents. We are to learn from the examples in it, obey the commands in it, and follow the guidelines in it. In doing so we not only serve as examples to our children, but we bring glory to God as well.

Keeping the Word of God as a frontlet between our eyes suggests the *presence* of the word. We are to keep it ever before us, out in front where we can see it, and let it be a reminder and a guide to us.

Do you remember the call of Moses? God wanted him to lead His people out of slavery in Pharaoh's Egypt. Moses was overwhelmed. Perhaps you feel the same way when you think of your responsibility as a parent. Despite forty years of the best training Egypt offered, Moses felt inadequate.

God's answer to Moses was all that he needed. He promised him His presence. "Certainly I will be with thee," He said (Exodus 3:12). Later in the life of Moses, at a time of great discouragement, God renewed that promise to him.

27

God will help you to be an effective, faithful parent, and if you are a believer, you have the promise of His presence. But look at what Paul wrote to the Colossians. "Let the word of Christ dwell in you richly in all wisdom" (Colossians 3:16). That is just like saying, "Let God's Word be a frontlet between your eyes." You have the assurance of God in your life, because His Spirit dwells in you. But does His Word dwell in you richly in all wisdom? If the presence of God gives confidence, the presence of His Word, dwelling in you richly, can multiply that confidence.

As a parent, you need to memorize the Word of God. You need to meditate on it regularly. You must let it dwell in you richly, and let it be as a frontlet before your eyes to remind you of God's presence and to give you guidance.

Binding the Scriptures on our arms signifies the practice of God's Word. Letting it be a frontlet before our eyes suggests the presence of God's Word. And writing it on our gates and doorposts shows the *prominence* of God's Word.

Parent, how prominent is the Word of God in your life? What is the testimony of your home to those that see it from the outside? Is the Word of God written on your gates and doorposts? I don't mean that you necessarily need to put a sign with a Scripture verse on your door. What I mean, and what I think Deuteronomy 6:9 teaches us, is that the testimony of God's Word should be so prominent in our lives and families that when an outsider sees us, one of the first things he should be able to tell is that our family reveres the Word of God.

What is the testimony of your life? What is the testimony of your family? Do you love the Word of God? Do you teach the Word of God? Do you keep the Word of God? If so, you are the kind of parent America needs.

A Christian home must have Christian parents who are sensitive to the Spirit of God and the Word of God. Perhaps you need to receive Christ as your Savior yourself. Perhaps you need to commit yourself to a new loving obedience to the Word of God. Will you not do it today?

1. Alvin Toffler, *Future Shock* (New York: Random House, 1970), pp. 216-17.
2. Ferdinand Lundberg, *The Coming World Transformation* (Garden City, NY: Doubleday, 1963), p. 295.

3

How to Fight the World— and Win!

Henrietta Mears correctly observed that God does not always choose great people to accomplish what He wishes, but He always chooses a person who is yielded to Him. Do you want God to use you as a parent to accomplish great things in the lives of your children? Then *you* must be yielded to Him.

In the eyes of the world a parent committed to Christ may not always be great. But in the eyes of the Lord, in the eyes of their children, and in the eyes of those who know them best, they are persons without equal. Their lives are marked by love and unselfish service.

But mothers and fathers in our times bear heavy burdens. The pressures against Christian homes have never been greater. Many wonder if they can counterattack or even hold the line. How can the Christian family resist today's heavy pressure to compromise biblical standards?

The *opposition* to the traditional family and its values today is overwhelming. But the *opportunities* for the family and for growth in the family are tremendous, too. As I study the New Testament, and especially the life of the Lord Jesus, I see three encouraging truths for today's Christian families.

The first truth that encourages me about today's families is *the pattern we have for living in a Christian home,* and that pattern is the Lord Himself in His submission.

Some time ago I read a short account of a very human happening. A family was planning a full-day treat for Mother on her birthday. She was to have the entire day to herself, to do whatever she wanted. The father and children would cook the meals and clean the house while Mother relaxed.

They had planned a picnic. The whole family would go to a nearby lake to spend the day. The son would join some friends in water skiing, and the daughter would play tennis. Mother could rest and read while father tried out the new fishing rod he had received for Christmas.

When the day arrived, however, the family was taken up with getting ready. So Mother got breakfast ready for everyone. Then, after she had helped them find their things and loaded the car, there was only enough room in the car for three.

That was all right, Mother said. She would not mind the day at home. She would have peace and quiet and probably get more accomplished than if she went to the lake. The family agreed. After all, Mom was only going to read and relax, and she could do that as well at home as at the lake. Maybe better.

While the family was gone, Mother tidied up the house a bit. She ironed her daughter's dress for that evening, picked up the father's suit at the cleaner, did a couple of loads of laundry, did a few other odds and ends that had needed doing for some time, fixed supper for the family, and even baked herself a birthday cake.

There were a few presents at Mother's plate for dinner, and everyone agreed that she was the greatest. Someone suggested that this was the nicest birthday she had ever had.

Mother, reflecting, had to agree that indeed it had been one of the nicest, most meaningful birthdays she could remember.

Why was that birthday such a special one? Because that mother derived her satisfaction in the family from her loving, submissive service to others.

Christ Himself was an example of that kind of service to others. Think for a moment what Christ came into this world to do. The world He entered at Bethlehem was black as night. Just as it does today, sin seemed to reign supreme and unchallenged. When Jesus was yet a little baby, Satan moved King Herod to try to take His life. As Jesus prepared to minister, the "establishment" was solidly against him—priesthood, government, and even the predominant attitude of the people. It seemed that everyone and everything was against Him.

But He "was the true Light" (John 1:9), and He shined in the darkness of those days. Remember who Jesus is. He is God (John 1:1), but He became man (John 1:14) and humbled Himself even to the point of dying on the cross for sins that He had not committed (Philippians 2:8). Jesus' entire life was marked by a humble service to others, and His example is our pattern for family living, whether we are mothers, fathers, or children.

Notice some significant observations we can make about the way our Lord approached the task that was before Him. First, He was totally yielded to the Father's will. "I seek not mine own will," He said in John 5:30, "but the will of the Father which hath sent me." His Father's will was seldom easy, but the Lord was determined to do it just the same. "My meat," He said, "is to do the will of him that sent me, and to finish his work" (John 4:34). His very sustenance was the Father's will. Obeying God was what kept Him going.

Second, to do God's will, He was submissive even to the ones who mistreated Him. Peter, who spent the entirety of

33

Christ's public ministry with Him, writes a remarkable thing in his first epistle. He says that when Jesus was reviled, He "reviled not again; when he suffered, he threatened not; but committed himself to him that judgeth righteously" (1 Peter 2:23). Jesus submitted Himself to others, even when they abused Him!

Look again at 1 Peter 2. Verse 21 says that Christ's sufferings and the way He responded to them were "an example, that ye should follow his steps." We are called and commanded to follow the same example of submission that Jesus showed, submitting to men and committing Himself to God.

Ephesians 5 makes the same point. Verse 21 says that we are to submit ourselves to one another in the fear of God.

No Christian family can be successful unless the example of submission is followed by every member. No other human relationship is as basic as that of the family. And unless submission is practiced in the family, the family relationships will fail. And if we fail in the relationships of the family, we will fail in every relationship of life.

The Moody Bible Institute sponsored family-life conferences across the nation for several years. In almost every conference the same problems surfaced in the families of those who responded. The problems began in relationships between members of the family, and they seemed universally to spread to other areas of life.

If I could sum up one great truth that would help a family make giant strides toward success in fighting both the internal and external pressures of today's world on the family, it would be this: learn the importance of loving, submissive service to one another.

Many magazines and books today are filled with counsel for parents and families. Some of it is constructive. But most of it is frighteningly destructive. Most of the advice falls short because it fails to recognize that most family conflict is essentially a spiritual problem. The real foes of the family today are not social change or even permissiveness. The real foes of the Christian family are the same as the foes of the Christian: the world, the flesh, and Satan himself, which all work together to stir up pride in the Christian. And the only answer to that pride is the loving, serving, submissive mind of Christ (Philippians 2:5-8).

THE POWER FOR THE CHRISTIAN HOME—JESUS' LIFE

A second truth that encourages me about the potential of Christian families today is *the power we have for living in a Christian home,* and that is the very life of Christ.

As God Himself, Jesus had unlimited power. Hebrews 1 tells us that He is the creator of the universe. His power is infinite. But did you know that while He was here on earth, Jesus did not use that power? Every miracle He ever did, every healing He ever performed, was done in the Father's power. Jesus said, "The Son can do nothing of himself" (John 5:19), and, "I can of mine own self do nothing" (John 5:30). Not only was Jesus yielded to the Father's will, but He was dependent on the Father's power as well.

Again and again, Jesus stressed the same important fact. "The words that I speak unto you I speak not of myself," He claimed, "but the Father that dwelleth in me, he doeth the works" (John 14:10).

By the same token, the Christian is not to live in his own power but in the power of Christ. The great apostle Paul, who did so much for the Lord, gave the secret of his effectiveness. "I am crucified with Christ," he wrote. "Nevertheless I live; yet not I, *but Christ liveth in me*: and the life which I now live in the flesh I live by the faith of the Son of God" (Galatians 2:20, italics added). The power for his life was not Paul's own, but it was the resurrection power of the Lord Jesus.

The truth that the Lord Jesus is the empowerment for the

35

Christian's life and obedience to God runs throughout the New Testament. Paul said, "I can do all things through Christ which strengtheneth me" (Philippians 4:13).

Parent, if you are a believer in Christ, you are not alone. Christ dwells in you through His Spirit, and He has promised that He will never leave you nor forsake you (Hebrews 13:5). He is your power to live and to lead your family. You have a tremendous task and an overwhelming responsibility. But God did not give it to you without the enablement to do it.

Are the influences of this world on your family more than you can handle? God does not expect you to handle them in your own power. But you, too, can do all things through Christ, who will strengthen you. He will be your power to have the kind of family that meets God's high standards.

THE PROMISE FOR THE CHRISTIAN HOME— CHRIST'S PRESENCE

A third truth that encourages me as I think about the tremendous opposition to and opportunity for the Christian family is *the promise we have for living in a Christian home.* I am speaking of the promise of Christ's presence. We have already seen Christ's promise in Hebrews 13:5. "I will never leave thee, nor forsake thee." Look now at another verse of Scripture. In Colossians 1:27, Paul writes that Christ in us is "the hope of glory."

John taught that Christ was the embodiment of God's glory. In John 1:14 he wrote, "And the Word was made flesh, and dwelt among us, (and we beheld his glory, the glory as of the only begotten of the Father,) full of grace and truth." Do you wish to have a family that reflects the glory of God? Do you want your family to live by God's grace and truth? Christ's presence among you is your hope, or promise, of the glory of God.

You can have a family that redounds to the glory of God if

you understand the truth of His presence. He is an unseen member of your family. He never sleeps or fails or falls short in His blessings. You are laborers together with Him, and your family is just a part of an even bigger family—the family of God.

What does His presence mean to your family? Does the knowledge that He is there affect what you talk about? What you watch on television? How you treat each other? How you treat guests in your home?

Are outsiders who come into contact with your family aware of His presence there? Is your home really different from other homes because of the presence of the Lord? Does His presence make your mealtimes different? Do you share together as a family in prayer and in God's Word?

And is Christ truly the head and the center of your family? Are you sensitive to His will, and do you seek His guidance? Is His Word the final authority in your family's decisions and disagreements?

If we truly recognize and respond to the presence of Christ in our families, it will make an impact on our daily lives.

But perhaps Christ is not in your family. Perhaps you have never really trusted Him as your Savior. "But as many as received him," says John 1:12, "to them gave he power to become the sons of God, even to them that believe on his name." Unless you have been born again, you are not in His family. And if you are not in His family, He is not in yours.

My friend, will you trust Him today and receive His offer of free forgiveness of sins? He died for your sins that you might live for Him, and He offers eternal life to you as a gift, freely, if you will accept it by faith (Romans 3:24-25).

Truly the family of today is suffering. Its exact status is in dispute. According to the 1976 report of the United States Census Bureau, more than 1,300,000 unmarried couples are living together in our country.

On the other hand, a lead article in the magazine *Changing Times* says that the picture is better than many think. "When the smoke clears," says the magazine, "most authorities expect that the family will still occupy the central position in most people's lives."[1] As proof, the article cited a survey of nearly 200,000 college freshmen at 366 schools across the country. Of these, more than half listed "raising a family" as one of the most important goals of their lives. Most put raising a family ahead of financial success and all other goals.[2]

If raising a family is such a priority in so many people's lives, why aren't they more successful at it? Because without Christ, there really is no hope for any family. Without His submission as our pattern we are left with our weakness and insufficiency. And without His presence as our promise, we are left with our hopelessness and confusion.

No family can be a success without Christ. How is your family doing?

1. "What Future for the American Family?" *Changing Times* 30, no. 12 (December 1976): 10.
2. Ibid., p. 9.

4

God's Pattern for Parents

The average family in America today enjoys a higher standard of living than ever before. However, there are many disturbing signs that the family faces serious problems. The failure of the home is a definite threat in our world today. Laymen and educators alike are expressing concern over the health of this basic institution of our society.

Dr. K. E. Appel of the University of Pennsylvania states that the family is in a state of serious crisis. And he suggests some reasons for the crisis.

First, he says, *the family is seriously fragmented.* It does not hold together any longer than circumstances compel it to do so. As long as it is expedient, or as long as the marriage satisfies selfish personal needs, it stays together, albeit sometimes only in name.

In this permissive age in which we live, some people look upon the institution of marriage simply as a convenient way for a man and a woman to live together. And if marriage is not convenient, often they live together anyway. The media seems to delight in publishing shocking statistics and predictions about marriage. For example, the *London Observer* printed a headline some time ago that asked, "Are We the Last Married Generation?" In the accompanying article, British psychologist James Heming, a member of England's official Marriage Guidance Council, predicted that engagements are doomed and weddings will soon be something of the past.

Of course we disagree with such predictions, but the fact that they are widely being made says something about the state of marriage.

The truth is that marriage is God's provision for the family, which He ordained from the beginning, even before Adam sinned. Some have always violated the biblical ideal of the family and marriage. But now God's structure and plan for the family is being neglected and ignored by many.

In an article in *Moody Monthly* magazine, Christian psychologist Dr. Lacey Hall reminds us, "The Christian needs to realize what is happening to the family if he is to understand the forces shaping his own home, his own children, the families in his church and the homes in his neighborhood."[1]

Second, Dr. Appel suggests that a reason for the crisis in the home is that *the average family is rootless,* having few ties of tradition or history. Since the beginning of the post-World-War II era, America has been on the move. Twenty percent of the population changes its place of residence annually. Industry and business demand people who will move. One third of all families with husbands under thirty-five years of age move each year.

Dr. Lacey Hall suggested that such mobility is changing the roots of the home. When the family moves, he said, it has to adjust to new housing, new schools, and new friends. And the strain that is put on the family relationships can lead to deep feelings of insecurity and instability. He quoted a book that compared such mobile families to young trees grown at a nursery with shallow roots for easy transplanting. Such trees, he said, cannot withstand the storms.[2] Many of today's families are not equipped to weather the storms of today's world.

As a result of all this rootlessness, many families today have lost all sense of orientation. Some wives really are not certain whether they want to be wives and mothers, husbands are not sure whether they want to be husbands and fathers, and children are not given the opportunity to experience childhood in a well-ordered and secure home.

Security is vital to a family. It seems obvious that the first requirement for a unified and happy family is a sense of belonging for every member. And yet, today's families have largely lost any sense of unity or security between family members. The result is a loss of harmony and an abundance of personal conflicts.

Many of the responsibilities that really belong in the home have been taken over by other agencies, such as the school, local clubs, and even the church. The result is that today families are made up of individuals who have little time for each other because their lives are so wrapped up in their own activities.

In many homes the husband, wife, and children all come and go as they please—often failing even to check in. In such an atmosphere genuine communication is impossible, and the family structure breaks down.

Yes, the family today is seriously in need of help.

And let's remember that although the Christian home is different, it is not automatically exempt from those problems. Even the Christian family is adversely affected by the many crises of our society. Never before has there been such a gaping need in the average Christian family as now.

Is there help for the Christian home today? What does God's Word say about it?

I am convinced that the only hope for the problems of any family is to be found in the Word of God. As I look at God's Word, I see three steps that must be taken by the parent who would follow God's pattern for family living.

REPENT OF YOUR SINS

Some time ago a mother shared with me her heartache concerning a married son who had committed suicide.

41

"Apples do not fall far from the trees," she said, as she spoke of the problems her son had experienced. She told how he had capped a fast romance with a speedy marriage. He had not had time to get to know his wife, and she had not had time to get to know him. Their romance and marriage had been too hasty. Potential problems had just been brushed over until after the honeymoon.

Soon his wife had discovered that he was a heavy drinker. He was emotionally immature, totally lacking any sense of responsibility. He was no more reliable than a cracked barometer. He was really a poor marriage risk!

But she had viewed marriage as a kind of reform school. She thought that after the wedding she could be a good influence on him and work on his faults. Needless to say, it did not work. Such an arrangement never works. It is the testimony of most married couples that after marriage a person's faults are the same, and often more intense.

Shortly after the birth of the couple's first child he deserted the family, and the marriage ended in divorce. Five years later he was dead—a victim of his own hand.

"He was just like his father," said the mother. "Apples do not fall far from the trees."

That mother's grim words reminded me of some fundamental Bible truths, especially that we always reap what we sow (Galatians 6:7). "Be sure your sin will find you out," says Numbers 32:23. You cannot sin without suffering the consequences of your sin. Therefore, if you want to follow God's pattern for the family, you must first *repent of your sins.*

The Old Testament book of Exodus tells about the children of Israel as they traveled through the wilderness. There, as they pitched their tents around Mt. Sinai, God gave them His immutable law. In explaining the very first commandment, God made this remarkable statement: "I the LORD thy God am a jealous God, visiting the iniquity of

42

the fathers upon the children unto the third and fourth generation of them that hate me" (Exodus 20:5).

Moses was so impressed by that statement that he repeated it in Exodus 34:7. And years later, when the children of Israel wavered between fervor and fear, Moses recalled those exact words in Deuteronomy 5:9. They were unforgettable to Moses. He had seen God write them upon the tables of stone, and they were indelibly etched also upon the table of his heart. Those words were terrifying then, and they are terrifying now! They mean that our children can reap the results of our sins unto the third and fourth generation.

Every second a baby is born into this world. They are emotionally, physically, and morally capable of developing into mature, happy, well-adjusted adults, by the grace and power of God. Yet most people grow up to become just the opposite—miserable, unhappy, and frustrated. Why? I am convinced that it is largely due to the sins of the parents.

God's Word says, "Be not deceived; God is not mocked: for whatsoever a man soweth, that shall he also reap. For he that soweth to his flesh shall of the flesh reap corruption; but he that soweth to the Spirit shall of the Spirit reap life everlasting" (Galatians 6:7-8). And we are not the only ones who reap the consequences of our sins; our children reap them also.

Yes, apples do not fall far from the trees. George Gordon, Lord Byron, the famous English poet, is an example of one who reaped the sins of his parents. Humanly speaking, he had everything going for him. He was handsome, witty, intelligent, and gifted—and yet his life was a tragedy. At the age of thirty-six he wrote his final poem:

> My days are in the yellow leaf;
> The flowers and fruit of Love are gone;
> The worm, the canker, and the grief
> Are mine alone!

Neither glacier, mountain, torrent,
Forest or cloud can lighten the weight
Upon my heart, or enable me to lose
My wretched identity.

                    "On This Day I Complete My
                    Thirty-Sixth Year"   [Stanza 2]

Byron's ancestors, as far back as they can be traced, were violent, passionate, and unrestrained in their morals. And Byron lived as his parents lived. He openly violated all standards of morality and righteousness. He inherited his parents' sins.

He left unforgettable poetry, but Lord Byron also left an unforgettable example of what happens to children whose spiritual welfare is neglected by careless parents. He died a tragic death at a young age.

But look again at Exodus 20:5. It says that the sins of the parents are visited to the third and fourth generation of *them that hate God*. It is my conviction that the grace of God is extended as well to the children of sinning parents who repent of their sins. Of course, the children are not automatically saved because of the faith of their parents, but many of the effects and judgments for their parents' sins are removed from them when the parents turn to God in repentance.

Do you want to do what you can to assure that your children will not have to suffer the effects of your sins? Repent—turn from your sin to the Lord and seek His forgiveness. Confess to your children any sins that you may have committed against them. And purpose to serve God both as an example to your children and as a minister to them. The Lord may use your life to help reverse some of the consequences of your sin on your children.

RETURN TO THE BIBLE

A second step that you can take to realign your family

with God's pattern is to *return to the Bible.* There is no easy way—no shortcut or magic formula—to build a happy home. God's Word is clear when it instructs parents to bring up their children in "the nurture and admonition of the Lord" (Ephesians 6:4). A successful home must be built on the foundation of the Word of God.

God instructed the parents of Israel to teach and instruct their children in the precepts of Jehovah. Deuteronomy 6:7 says, "Thou shalt teach them *diligently* unto thy children" (italics added). The diligent teaching of the Word of God is the fundamental requirement for a successful, God-honoring home. It is God's plan for the family. The reading, studying, and memorizing of God's Word are essentials that cannot be overlooked.

A family that is not built on the foundation of God's Word will not stand. But you cannot hope to bring your family into focus with God's Word unless your own life is already meeting the standard. Repenting from past sins is good, but it is not enough. You must determine to obey God's Word from now on. You must be the example of obedience to God in your family.

And if you are to teach your family the Word of God, you must know it. Too many parents are biblically illiterate. Do you study God's Word regularly? If not, you will not be much of a teacher to your children.

RESPOND TO THE LORD

A third step to take in bringing your family into harmony with God's pattern is to *respond to the Lord.* Be sensitive to the will and direction of the Lord in your life. Parents, of course, must set a good example for their children to follow. Proverbs 22:6 says, "Train up a child in the way he should go: and when he is old, he will not depart from it."

The Old Testament tells us about Absalom, the third son of David. He was a man who had every opportunity to become something for God. But his father was not a good example to him. When David fell into sin with Bathsheba, Absalom surely knew about it. Apparently, that one poor example was enough to undo all David's prior teaching and example. Absalom reflected David's desire for self-gratification. Law meant nothing to him. He lived only for what he could get in the way of immediate results.

Absalom killed his brother for ravishing his sister. Then he conspired to overthrow his father, David. As David's soldiers went out after him, David pleaded with them to deal gently with the boy. But Absalom died in his rebellion—a victim of the sins of his parents.

Others in the Bible show the danger of parental insensitivity to the Lord. The sons of Noah, the daughters of Lot, the children of Jacob, of Eli, and of Samuel all give examples of the folly of failing to respond to the Lord.

Parent, if you are not sensitive and submissive to the will of God, your children will follow your example. They will be unresponsive to your authority as well as to God's. That is the natural law of sowing and reaping.

Are you willing to repent of your sin, return to the Bible, and respond to the Lord? Does the spiritual well-being of your family mean that much to you? It is a price to pay—or rather, seed to be sown. And you will reap the fruit of whatever seed you sow.

Remember the assessment of Dr. Appel? He said that family problems are caused by fragmentation in the family, by a lack of family roots, and by a lack of communication. Repentance from sin is the only way to heal the conflicts caused by fragmentation. A return to the Bible is the only way to restore the sense of solidity and stability caused by the loss of our roots. And a proper response to the Lord is the only answer to the loss of harmony caused by the breakdown in communication that has taken place in our families—because God's love and forgiveness are the only answers to the broken relationships and shattered bonds in our families. What will your response be?

1. Cited in "The Christian Home," by Gene A. Getz, Moody Manna Series (Chicago-Moody, 1967), p. 1
2. Lacey Hall, "What's Happening to the American Family?" *Moody Monthly* 67 (July-August 1967): 26
3. Ibid.

5

Train Up a Child

Horticulturist Luther Burbank warned long ago, "If we had paid no more attention to our plants than we have to our children, we would now be living in a jungle of weeds." Unfortunately there are many homes in our world today that resemble jungles instead of gardens. Juvenile delinquency continues to rise as parents are forced to reap what they have sown.

To bring up a child in this world is a tremendous responsibility. There is no bigger job than that of being a faithful and dedicated parent. The rearing of our children is one of the most important jobs we will ever engage in. We must do it carefully and prayerfully.

Dr. Payson said, "What if God should place a diamond in your hand and tell you to inscribe on it a sentence which should be read at the last day and shown there as an index of your thoughts and feelings. What care, what caution you would exercise in the selection!" That is exactly what God has done. He has placed before you the immortal minds of your children, less perishable than the diamond, on which you are inscribing every day and every hour by your instruction, by your spirit, by your example, something that will remain and be exhibited for you or against you at the judgment!

And yet, in spite of the tremendous responsibility, many parents today leave the instruction of their children to chance. Recently a brokenhearted father confessed to me, "I've spent more time training my dog than I have my sons." What a tragedy!

Many of the ten thousand runaway children in this country each year can be traced to homes in which little parental love and concern was demonstrated. Almost all juvenile delinquency is the result of parental neglect. A juvenile court judge in New York said, "When I retire I'm going to write a book and call it *Why I Hate Parents.*" Asked why he said that, he replied, "Because of my disgust with parental failure to assume their primary job—the care of their children."

A youth in Chicago who has already been in trouble with the law stated, "The only reason I know what my mother's face looks like is because my family gets together on Thursday evenings for one hour—from seven to eight P.M. The rest of the week, my mom and dad are running a thousand directions." No activity that robs children of parental care and companionship, no matter how important that activity might seem, is worthwhile.

God has ordained the family structure as we know it, and one of its primary purposes is for the training of children. Proverbs 22:6 clearly shows a parent's responsibility to his child. "Train up a child in the way he should go," it says, "and when he is old, he will not depart from it." *You* must teach them. You cannot leave the job to the school, the church, or the babysitter. It is your responsibility as a parent.

There are at least three character qualities that you must teach your children if when they are old they are to follow the way you have taught them.

Teach Your Children to Be Diligent

First, you should teach your children to be *diligent*. A leading law enforcement officer of a previous decade charged our society with substituting indulgence for discipline, pleasure for duty, and money for morals. As one who dealt with criminals and knew the criminal mind, he placed the blame for the growing menace of youth crime largely at the door of the parents. He cited as the heart of the problem parental "negligence, indifference, personal greed, and bad example." His words ring true today as we see an even further deterioration of the family.

In his book *Rome, Its Rise and Fall,* Phillip Van Ness Myers speaks of the disintegration of the Roman family as part of the reason for that great empire's collapse. Myers wrote, "The typical Roman family consisted of the father . . . and mother, the sons, together with their wives and sons, and the unmarried daughters. . . . The most important element or feature of this family group was the authority of the father."[1]

The historian continues, "It would be difficult to overestimate the influence of this group upon the history and destiny of Rome. It was the cradle of at least some of those splendid virtues of the early Romans that contributed to the strength and greatness of Rome, and that helped to give her the dominion of the world."[2]

But something happened. The stability of Roman family life did not last. By the end of the second century, Roman fathers, says Myers, had "yielded to the impulse to become far too complacent. Having yielded the habit of controlling their children, they let the children govern them, and took pleasure in bleeding themselves white to gratify the expensive whims of their offspring. The result was that they were succeeded by a generation of idlers and wastrels."[3] They failed to teach their children diligence.

Parents, you must teach your children diligence both by example and by precept. Teach them diligence in their responsibilities in the home, in the neighborhood, and at school. Teach them diligence in prayer. Teach them diligence in the study of God's Word. Teach them diligence in all things.

I am convinced that laziness and a lack of sense of purpose among today's young people are the greatest causes of their personal problems. If you have not taught your children to work, you have not taught them anything of value.

Eli is an example of a man who failed to teach his sons diligence. He was the high priest and a judge of Israel, and his sons worked in the Tabernacle. Or rather they occupied their time in the Tabernacle, supervising the offerings. First Samuel 2:12-14 tells us that they had devised an unlawful method of taking the people's sacrifices for their own personal use.

Those sons had followed the example of their lazy father and gone even further in their evil. They were desecrating the very sacrifices it was their duty to oversee. Eli had failed to teach them diligence.

God spoke through a prophet to Eli, condemning him for his failure to train his sons in the way they should go. "Wherefore kick ye at my sacrifice and at mine offering, which I have commanded in my habitation; and honourest thy sons above me, to make yourselves fat with the chiefest of all the offerings of Israel my people?" (1 Samuel 2:29). God blamed Eli for the sin he had allowed his sons to commit, and He said that it was really idolatry, or honoring Eli's own sons above God!

Failing to teach your children diligence is a serious sin against God as well as against your own children.

TEACH YOUR CHILDREN TO BE OBEDIENT

In our permissive society with its emphasis on children's rights, we seem to have forgotten that the child's direct command from God is to honor and obey his parents. And it is your responsibility to your child to teach him to be *obedient*. Obedience does not come naturally. Rebellion does, but obedience must be taught to a child from the very earliest age. And, parent, the responsibility to teach your children obedience falls not on the teacher, not on the babysitter, not on the neighbors, not on your youth pastor, but on you.

The apostle Paul, under the direction of the Holy Spirit, wrote, "Children, obey your parents in all things; for this is well-pleasing unto the Lord" (Colossians 3:20). Why should children obey? Because the Bible teaches that it is well pleasing unto the Lord. God is pleased with obedience. But there is another reason. Obedience will be necessary all through their lives. My dear father would often say to his six children, "Children, learn to obey the laws of this home, and the laws of the school, state, nation, and God will be easy to obey." Obedience to authority pleases God not just in the case of children in the home but for employees on the job, for citizens under the government, for students in a school, and even for members of a church.

In Ephesians 6:1 we read, "Children obey your parents in the Lord: for this is right." Why should children obey? Because it is right. Built into every divine and human institution are patterns of authority. Everyone, no matter what his position in life, is under authority. It is God's order. "The powers that be are ordained of God" (Romans 13:1). Obedience is right.

Luke 2:51 tells us that Jesus was subject to His parents in all things. If Jesus, the eternal Son of God, was subject to His earthly mother and father, surely it is right for every child to obey his parents.

In order to learn obedience a child needs discipline at times. The Bible emphasizes that. "He that spareth his rod hateth his son: but he that loveth him chasteneth him betimes" (Proverbs 13:24). "Chasten thy son while there is hope, and let not thy soul spare for his crying" (Proverbs 19:18). "Foolishness is bound in the heart of a child; but the rod of correction shall drive it far from him" (Proverbs 22:15).

The writer of the book of Hebrews calls attention to the same truth. "Now no chastening for the present seemeth to be joyous, but grievous," he writes. "Nevertheless, afterward it yieldeth the peaceable fruit of righteousness unto them which are exercised thereby" (Hebrews 12:11).

Someone has said that everything in the modern home is controlled by switches these days—except the children. The predominant feeling seems to be that children must not be restrained but given free release of their impulses. Some say that restraint may cause the child severe damage in his personality.

Dr. Jules Henry, a prominent St. Louis sociologist and author of *Culture Against Man* (New York: Random Vintage, 1963), charges that our society's permissiveness has turned our nation from being parent-centered to being child-centered. He correctly points out that permissiveness "leads to the destruction of gratitude and the elimination of guilt." Even more serious, "Where there is no concept of punishment," he says, "there is no concept of right or evil."

In debunking the theory that restraint harms a child, the doctor points out that most of the men who have been great leaders throughout history grew up in environments of strict discipline. Most of our own country's founders and leaders, he says, "grew up under firm fathers and mothers and under teachers whose prime pedagogical instrument was the birch rod."

Dr. Henry carefully explains that he is not calling for the "cat-o'-nine-tails and the straight jacket" treatment, but, said he, "There is a strange confusion nowadays in the minds of parents between authoritarianism and authority, and hand-in-hand with this confusion had gone the notion that the old-fashioned firm and commanding parent was somehow psychopathogenic."

It is my conviction that most youngsters, even those who are rebellious against adult authority, are actually seeking a strong hand of guidance. Discipline that sets definite boundaries of right and wrong for a child, discipline that demands his obedience, actually is a source of security to him. Several years ago the *New York Mirror* listed ten suggestions for parents who would like to take measures against juvenile delinquency. All of the suggestions were offered by boys who had been in trouble with the law. Paraphrased, they are:

1. Don't always give us our way.
2. Be firm but fair in discipline.
3. Make us feel wanted.
4. Teach us to work and get along with others.
5. Deal with and punish infractions of the family rules.
6. Listen to our side in arguments.
7. Carefully monitor our friends.
8. Don't let us stay out late at night.
9. Don't spare the rod.
10. Give more time to family-centered activities.

Eli failed in this respect, too. He did not teach his sons obedience. First Samuel, chapter 2, tells us that his sons were defiling the Tabernacle by having illicit relations with the women that assembled there. In response to such a great evil, Eli offered his sons a weak rebuke. "Nay, my sons," he said in verse 24. "It is no good report that I hear: ye make the LORD's people to transgress."

Eli's sons were grown men, but their attitude and behavior show that they had not learned obedience in their childhood. And if Eli's words to them are any indication of how he dealt with them as children, it is no wonder. He rebuked them, but he did not demand their obedience. He did not take steps to see that they were corrected, and he failed in his responsibility both as a father and as the high priest.

You can teach your children diligence and obedience and still fail in your greatest responsibility. You must teach them to be *reverent*. You must teach them to honor the Lord, His Word, and His ways.

Diligence is your child's responsibility to himself, and obedience is his responsibility to others, but reverence is his responsibility to the Lord, and that is the greatest responsibility of all.

Reverence is not just praying before meals. It is not just attending church regularly. It is not just reading the Bible or talking about spiritual things. It includes all those things, but it is more.

True reverence grows out of a heart devoted to the Lord. Genuine reverence is possible only in one who is a child of God. And your first step if you would teach your children reverence is to lead them to personal faith in the Lord Jesus Christ.

A disturbing thing in many Christian families today is that mothers and fathers are afraid or uneasy in talking freely to their children about the things of the Lord. Read Deuteronomy 6:6-9 about the parents' responsibility to speak freely of the things of the Lord and teach them to the children. We ought to instruct and encourage our children in the things of the Lord in every situation of life.

Look at some biblical examples of godly parents. Abraham was the friend of God, the Bible tells us. And God said of him, "I know him, that he will command his children and his household after him, and they shall keep the way of the LORD, to do justice and judgment" (Genesis 18:19). Abraham did not fail in his responsibility to teach his family reverence for the ways of the Lord, and look at the beautiful illustration of obedience and submission we have in Isaac, who allowed his father to bind him and place him on the altar of sacrifice!

Joshua led his entire family in the way of righteousness. He said, "As for me and my house, we will serve the LORD" (Joshua 24:15). He correctly assumed the responsibility for the spiritual leadership of his children.

Cornelius also "feared God with all his house" (Acts 10:2). His was one of the first Gentile families God brought into the church, and the testimony of his family's acceptance by God made great progress in the uniting of the Jewish and Gentile factions of the church.

But here again, Eli failed in his responsibility. As high priest in Israel, he had a position of spiritual leadership over the entire nation. But he could not even fulfill his spiritual responsibility to his own family! He failed to teach his sons reverence.

First Samuel 4 tells of the culmination of the sins of Eli's sons. Because they had not been taught diligence, they had desecrated the offerings of God. Because they had not been taught obedience, they had defiled the Tabernacle of God. And now, because they had not been taught reverence, they despised the Ark of God.

The Philistines had defeated Israel in a battle, and the irreverent, superstitious sons of Eli took the Ark of the Covenant into battle. The Ark belonged in the Most Holy Place in the Tabernacle, and even the high priest was not to enter there except once a year on the Day of Atonement. The Ark symbolized the presence of God and was the dwelling place of God's glory.

But Eli's sons had never learned reverence for the things of God. They intruded into the Holy of Holies and took the Ark with them into battle. As a result they were killed, the Ark was taken, and the glory of the Lord departed from Israel.

Parents, our task is immense, our responsibility is great. May God give us the wisdom and strength to do our job well. We must set an example of diligence, obedience, and reverence to God in all phases of our lives.

Does the thought of your responsibility overwhelm you? Look to God for the strength and wisdom to fulfill it. Make Christ the Lord of your life and of your family, and begin to train up your children in the way that they should go.

1. Phillip Van Ness Myers, *Rome, Its Rise and Fall* (Philadelphia: Richard West, 1901), pp. 11-12.
2. Ibid.
3. Ibid.

6

Handmaid of the Lord: A Mother Chosen by God

One of the fundamental doctrines of Christianity is that Jesus existed from eternity past. John 1:1 tells us that He "was God." Do not ever get the idea that His origin was at His conception in Nazareth. That was merely the beginning of His life on earth. As the Son of God, the second Member of the Trinity, He had always existed.

Hebrews 1 tells us that Jesus was at work in the creation of the world. He "laid the foundation of the earth; and the heavens are the works of [His] hands" (Hebrews 1:10). But He came into this world "to seek and to save that which was lost" (Luke 19:10). He was "made flesh" (John 1:14) that He might dwell among us and die for us.

God could have chosen any woman in the world to be the earthly mother of Jesus. But He chose Mary. Have you ever wondered why? She was a unique person, the one among millions that God selected to bring His Son into the world. She was blessed of God and highly favored. I believe the reason God chose her can be traced to three outstanding characteristics in her life.

PURITY THAT GREW OUT OF A CHASTE LIFE

First, Mary demonstrated *the purity that grows out of a chaste life.* The village of Nazareth, where Mary lived and grew up, lay in the path of the caravans that traveled from Capernaum to the seaports. As in every generation, there undoubtedly were women in that town who became involved with the traveling men. But not Mary. Mary was pure.

Of course there could not have been unfaithfulness of any kind in Mary. Otherwise God could not have chosen her. The words that came to her from Gabriel echoed full approval. "Fear not, Mary: for thou hast found favour with God" (Luke 1:30). Some of the great masterpieces of art that picture this great event show the angel presenting Mary with a lily. The lily symbolizes Mary's purity.

Luke 1:27 says that Mary was a virgin. I know that there are many today who reject that teaching. They attempt to do away with the supernatural reality of Christ's birth by suggesting that Jesus was born of a natural, human union. But to deny the virgin birth of Jesus is plainly to call God a liar.

Centuries before the angel appeared to Mary, the prophet Isaiah had written, "Therefore the Lord himself shall give you a sign; Behold, a virgin shall conceive, and bear a son, and shall call his name Immanuel" (Isaiah 7:14). God through His holy Word required that the mother of the Messiah would be a virgin—pure, chaste, and holy.

Luke goes to great lengths to defend the doctrine of the virgin birth. He states that she was a virgin (1:27); then he quotes Mary's own statement that she was a virgin (1:34); and then he reports the angel's confirmation that she was a virgin (1:35-37). Luke understood that the doctrine of Christ's virgin birth was essential to the Christian faith. For without the virgin birth we have not only an impure Mary, but a human Jesus and a faulty Bible as well.

His supernatural birth through a chaste virgin was necessary for the sinlessness of the holy Son of God.

When Mary received the angel's announcement, she was

overwhelmed. "How shall this be," she said, "seeing I know not a man?" (Luke 1:34). Mary was engaged to Joseph (Luke 1:27), but they had not yet come together as husband and wife. Imagine her amazement when the angel told her that she was to have a child!

The angel reassured her. "The Holy Ghost shall come upon thee," he said, "and the power of the Highest shall overshadow thee: therefore also that holy thing which shall be born of thee shall be called the Son of God" (Luke 1:35).

Then the angel gave Mary proof that her child would be without a human father. What was the proof? "Thy cousin Elisabeth, she hath also conceived a son in her old age; and this is the sixth month with her, who was called barren. For with God nothing shall be impossible" (Luke 1:36-37).

What was the angel saying? That if God could cause Elisabeth to conceive, He could do anything. If Elisabeth and Zacharias could have a child at their age, Mary could have a child without a human father. Nothing is too hard for the Lord.

Mary went to visit her cousin. When Mary and Elisabeth met, Elisabeth knew immediately that Mary was singularly blessed of the Lord. "When Elisabeth heard the salutation of Mary," Luke tells us, "the babe leaped in her womb; and Elisabeth was filled with the Holy Ghost: and she spake out with a loud voice, and said, blessed art thou among women, and blessed is the fruit of thy womb. And whence is this to me, that the mother of my Lord should come unto me?" (Luke 1:41-43).

This is yet another testimony to the purity of Mary. Elisabeth's blessing was an acknowledgement that her chaste, pure cousin was indeed blessed by God to be the human mother of His Son.

But to say that Mary was pure is not to say that she was any different from you or me in regard to her sin nature. Mary was not sinless. Jesus was, but not Mary. She was a person just like you and me. She, like all human beings had "sinned, and come short of the glory of God" (Romans 3:23). To be sure, she was pure, chaste, and holy, but only because she had responded to God in faith. We do not worship Mary; we worship her Son, who alone is sinless.

Submission That Grew Out of a Humble Heart

Another significant characteristic in the life of Mary that led to God's choosing her was *the submission that grows out of a humble heart.*

Luke tells us that "the angel came in unto her, and said, Hail, thou that art highly favoured, the Lord is with thee: blessed art thou among women" (Luke 1:28). What was Mary's response to such a blessing? "She was troubled at his saying, and cast in her mind what manner of salutation this should be" (Luke 1:29).

What would your response have been to such praise from an angel? What would mine have been? We probably would have been flattered. But Mary was troubled and confused. She was humbled.

I want you to notice her amazing humility. When the angel finished his startling announcement that she was to be the mother of the Messiah, she beautifully replied, "Behold the handmaid of the Lord; be it unto me according to thy word" (Luke 1:38). What a beautiful response! "Lord, I'm your servant. Whatever You want, I want." What submission! Mary could have hesitated or even rebelled. But she did not.

Have you ever considered what it cost Mary to be the mother of Jesus? It cost her her reputation. It almost cost her Joseph.

Think of what Mary must have felt. *What will I tell people, since I have no husband? And what will I tell Joseph?* How overwhelmed she must have been!

But also think of what Joseph must have thought. When

he heard about Mary, he must have been disturbed by doubt. Mary had not told him how she had come to be in this condition. From Matthew's account, we learn just how upset Joseph was. Matthew 1:19 states, "Joseph . . . being a just man, and not willing to make her a publick example, was minded to put her away privily." Joseph, himself being a righteous man, was going to divorce her quietly, as was his prerogative under the law.

But God intervened, and "while he thought on these things, behold, the angel of the Lord appeared unto him in a dream, saying, Joseph, thou son of David, fear not to take unto thee Mary thy wife: for that which is conceived in her is of the Holy Ghost" (Matthew 1:19-20).

Joseph was satisfied, but what do you think Mary's neighbors thought? And what do you think the relatives thought? How much abuse do you think Mary suffered because of her submission to the Lord?

What else did it cost Mary to obey the Lord? Look at the prophecy of Simeon. When Jesus was just eight days old, His parents took Him to the Temple to be dedicated. In the Temple there was an old devout man by the name of Simeon, who had received a promise from the Holy Spirit that he would not die before he saw the Messiah. When he saw the baby Jesus, he knew that the promise had been fulfilled. He turned to Mary and said, "Behold, this child is set for the fall and rising again of many in Israel; and for a sign which shall be spoken against; (Yea, a sword shall pierce through thy own soul also,) that the thoughts of many hearts may be revealed" (Luke 2:34-35).

How was a sword to pierce through the soul of Mary? Imagine how she must have felt when she saw the multitudes reject and ridicule her son. What do you think she felt when He was accused of being demonic and in league with Satan? And imagine what must have gone through her heart as she stood by and watched Him be crucified. She saw them drive the nails into His hands, she saw His beaten and battered face, and she heard His cries from the cross. Surely a sword pierced through her soul!

Yes, it cost Mary a great deal to be submissive to God. Think also of the inconvenience to both Mary and Joseph. Not only were they talked about and persecuted, but some time after the birth of Jesus, they were forced to take Him to Egypt to avoid an attempt by Herod to kill Him. Mary and Joseph were never wealthy. When Jesus was dedicated at the Temple, they had to offer the offering of the poor (Luke 2:24). Even in His death, the Lord had to make provision for Mary so that she could live after He was gone. She was too poor to live without outside help (John 19:26-27). She had paid a very great price for her obedience to God.

And yet isn't that the same submissive spirit the Lord demands in all of us?

DEVOTION THAT GREW OUT OF A DEDICATED MIND

Finally, I see in Mary *the devotion that grows out of a dedicated mind.* Mary knew her Bible. And she loved the Word of God. Although she was very young, possibly still in her teens, Mary was a devout person. She knew the Scriptures well. She had studied the Law and the Prophets.

Her song, which we know as "The Magnificat," refers to portions of Scripture from 1 Samuel, the Psalms, Isaiah, Micah, and Exodus. It is a very beautiful passage.

> And Mary said, My soul doth magnify the Lord, and my spirit hath rejoiced in God my Saviour. For he hath regarded the low estate of his handmaiden: for, behold, from henceforth all generations shall call me blessed. For he that is mighty hath done to me great things; and holy is his name. And his mercy is on them that fear him from generation to generation. He hath showed strength with his arm; he hath scattered the proud in the imagination of their

64

hearts. He hath put down the mighty from their seats, and exalted them of low degree. He hath filled the hungry with good things; and the rich he hath sent empty away. He hath holpen his servant Israel, in remembrance of his mercy; as he spake to our fathers, to Abraham, and to his seed for ever. [Luke 1:46-55]

What a beautiful expression of faith, coming out of a mind totally dedicated to the Lord! It is true that Mary could have been given those words, without any forethought on her part, by divine inspiration. But I believe that they came out of her life of familiarity with the Word of God. What she had studied and pondered in her heart broke out in glorious praise. Mary had saturated her mind and life with the Scriptures. Her mind was full of the treasure of the Word of God.

What makes me think so? Because as I see the life of Mary I notice that one of her outstanding characteristics was her inclination to ponder the things of God. She was not an idle talker. She was not a waster of time. Because she came from an environment of poverty, she had to work hard to see that the needs of the family were met. But she spent her spare time meditating on the things of the Lord.

Remember the story of when Jesus' parents went to Jerusalem for the Passover? They left, and no one noticed that Jesus, who was just a boy at the time, was not with the group. When they returned and found Jesus in the Temple, He asked, "How is it that ye sought me? wist ye not that I must be about my Father's business?" (Luke 2:49).

Jesus' parents, the Bible tells us, did not understand the meaning of His words. The account concludes with this poignant statement: "But his mother kept all these sayings in her heart" (Luke 2:51). What a privilege was hers, to be so intimately related to the Son of God! And Mary treasured up all His words and meditated on them. She was a devout, modest, worshiping mother.

Why did God select Mary? We have seen three reasons. He chose her for her purity and chaste life. He chose her for her submission and humble heart. And He chose her for her devotion and dedicated mind.

Think about those same three characteristics in terms of the Lord Jesus. He was pure. Hebrews 7:26 tells us that He was "holy, harmless, undefiled, separate from sinners." It is the consistent teaching of Scripture that Jesus was totally pure and without sin. He was also submissive. Philippians 2:8 tells us that He became obedient unto death. His submission was total. And He was devoted. He rose up early to pray. He said that His meat was to do the Father's will. His devotion to the Father was total.

It is interesting to think that the One who was totally pure, totally submissive, and totally devoted to God the Father saw examples of those same three characteristics in His earthly mother from the time He was an infant. She was a good mother for the One who was God in the flesh.

And Mary is an example of the kind of mothers we need today.

We need mothers who will teach their children purity, submission, and devotion. We need mothers who will be examples to their children. We need mothers like Mary.

And yet, let us not forget that Mary, too, was a person with needs. She was a woman in need of a Savior (Luke 1:47). And she recognized her need. Mary will be in heaven not because Jesus was her child, but because Jesus was her Savior, Lord, and Redeemer. Is He yours?

7

Hannah: The Mother Behind God's Man

We are living in a changing world!

Motherhood, the American flag, and apple pie used to be known for their stability and nationwide appeal. Today, however, the price of apples is up, the flag is down, and motherhood is abused.

Yes, motherhood has fallen on hard times. Television makes fun of mothers, children often treat their own mothers with scorn and contempt, and even many women these days ridicule the old values of the housewife and mother. Career-minded, "liberated" young women are admired and respected in our society, and motherhood is not even considered as an option by many young girls.

But we have a need today for mothers who will guide and guard the home. It is a high and holy calling and one with much potential for great influence either for good or for evil. Motherhood is a tremendous responsibility.

Good mothers are the key to happy homes and a great nation. Through the years, the mother has been a stabilizing force in the shaping of history. Several years ago, a nationwide survey was conducted by the University of Michigan. Thousands of girls between the ages of eleven and eighteen were questioned regarding their personal and social ambitions. When asked what they would like to be in adult life, a surprising 80 percent expressed a desire to be like their mothers.

It has been said many times that no other force in the life of a son is as strong as the influence of a mother, and the testimony of millions of sons bears this out. Napoleon said, "The future destiny of the child is always the work of the mother. Let France have good mothers and she is bound to have good sons."

"The mother is the one supreme asset of the national life," said President Theodore Roosevelt. "She is more important by far than the successful statesman, businessman, artist, or scientist."

Many famous men have been greatly influenced by their mothers. George Washington's mother was a patriotic and religious woman. Her son became the father of his country. Lord Bacon's mother was a woman of superior intelligence and deep piety. He reflected her character in his own. Sir Walter Scott's mother was a great lover of poetry and literature. He became one of the finest poets of all time.

In contrast, Byron's mother was proud, contentious, and violent. He became a social misfit and died at a young age. Nero's mother was greedy, lustful, and a murderess. He became one of the worst tyrants and mass murderers the world has ever seen. Without a doubt mothers influence their children for good or for evil.

So often the traits of the mother are passed on to the children! Children learn by observation, and they learn mostly from their mothers, because they have more time to observe their mothers than anyone else.

Susannah Wesley was a great Christian mother. Despite the fact that she had nineteen children, she found time to give each child an hour's religious instruction each week. She taught her children to love God and to honor the Bible. One of her sons, John Wesley, became the founder of the Methodist movement. Another of her sons, Charles Wesley, was one of the most prolific hymnwriters the church has ever seen. His songs are a heritage the church enjoys widely today, and both Charles and John claimed that they owed a great deal to their mother.

No less a man than Abraham Lincoln said, "All that I am, or can become, I owe to my angel mother." What a tribute!

In the Old Testament, in 1 Samuel 1, we see a beautiful picture of a good mother. Hannah lived in a day when, as a nation, Israel was in bad shape. The conditions closely resembled the corruption and disorder of today. The nation's leaders had failed. Gideon and Samson, the spiritual leaders, were nothing more than memories. Patriotism was nil and morals were low. The heroes were all dead, and the prophets were yet unborn. The nation was stumbling, and a spiritual rebirth was desperately needed.

Hannah, we are told, came from a little town called Ramathaim-zophim. It was just a wide spot in the road. The biggest thing about it was its name. And yet in that little obscure village, God had a mother. And He would eventually have His servant.

God so often uses the small people of this world to bring about His divine purposes! And so it was with Hannah. God would take this obscure woman, build her character through trials and hardships, and use her to have an instrumental part in His dealings with the entire nation.

The influence of Hannah is still felt today. She was a great mother, and her story is an inspiration to mothers everywhere. There are three events in her life that show her greatness as a mother.

HER PRAYER

The first event in the life of Hannah that demonstrates her greatness as a mother is her *prayer*. Hannah was a praying woman. She was a woman of sorrow. She had been denied the crowning glory of every Hebrew woman—the privilege of motherhood. She was childless. For years she had prayed for a son. She longed to take her own son to Shiloh on the yearly pilgrimage to the Tabernacle for worship. And now, still with no child, her disappointment was more than she could bear.

The Scriptures tell us that she was deeply disturbed. She came from a devoted but divided family. They went to worship at the Tabernacle every year at the appointed time (1 Samuel 1:3). But there was not harmony in the home. Elkanah, Hannah's husband, had another wife. Polygamy was sometimes practiced in Old Testament times, but it was a violation of God's principles. Jesus made clear that from the beginning it was God's design that one man should marry one woman and that they should remain married (Matthew 19:3-6). Those who violate God's principles of marriage suffer the consequences, sometimes in strained relationships.

And the relationship in Elkanah's home were severely strained. Peninnah, Elkanah's other wife, teased Hannah because of Hannah's childlessness (1 Samuel 1:6). Hannah "was in bitterness of soul," the Bible tells us in 1 Samuel 1:10, "and [she] prayed unto the LORD, and wept sore."

Hannah's response to Peninnah's teasing was not a personal attack, but prayer to the Lord. She was a devout, godly, praying woman, and she turned to the Lord in earnest, fervent prayer.

Here was a woman totally yielded to God! First Samuel 1:7 tells us that her desire for a son was so great that while they were at the Tabernacle she gave up eating to pray. She prayed with tears, and she prayed silently. Her prayers were so intense that Eli, the high priest, thought that she was drunk! Her lips were moving, but no sound was coming out (1 Samuel 1:13), and as Eli watched the intensity of expression and anguish on her face, as he saw her lips moving and the tears running down her face, he thought she must be drunk.

That says something to me about Hannah's dedication. Even the high priest in those days of spiritual drought could not tell the difference between devotion and drunkenness! Apparently he had never seen anyone pray with such fervor, and that is a sad statement on the spiritual climate of those days.

Hannah refused to let the spiritual atmosphere around her be the determiner of her consecration to the Lord. Eli's wicked sons ran the Tabernacle and had made it a place of immorality and thievery. But Hannah came, unaffected by all the corruption around her, and poured out her heart to God in prayer.

Here was Hannah, just a simple woman from a simple family in a small village, coming to Shiloh, then the spiritual capital of Israel, to seek the Lord in prayer. And her dedication to the Lord and the faith that she evidenced made her head and shoulders above anyone else in the nation. And God was to use her in a very great way.

HER PROMISE

A second event in Hannah's life that shows her greatness as a mother is her *promise*. Look at Hannah's promise to the Lord in 1 Samuel 1:11. "And she vowed a vow, and said, O LORD of hosts, if thou wilt indeed look on the affliction of thine handmaid, and remember me, and not forget thine handmaid, but wilt give unto thine handmaid a man child, then will I give him unto the LORD all the days of his life, and there shall no razor come upon his head."

Hannah's desire for a son was not just for what she could get out of it. She longed for a son, but she longed for a son that she could dedicate to the Lord. With the eyes of faith, she saw what God could do with a small child dedicated to Him. And she wanted a son—not to bring glory to herself, but to bring glory to God.

71

Her request was for a man child. She did not want just a healthy child, but specifically a boy. Why? A girl would have sufficed if all she wanted was to stop Peninnah's mocking. But that was not Hannah's primary motive in asking for a child. She wanted a child who could serve God by working in the Tabernacle, and only a boy would do.

Yes, Hannah had plans for this boy. He would be God's child, not hers and Elkanah's. He would serve in the Tabernacle and work for God all the days of his life. Furthermore, he would live the life of a Nazirite all his life.

A Nazirite was a man who had taken a vow to serve the Lord and be set apart especially for Him. Numbers 6 tells us the requirements for a Nazirite. He would be separate from wine and strong drink. In fact he would not eat grapes, raisins, or any other product of the grapevine. He would not shave his head or allow a razor to touch the locks of his hair. And he would not touch any dead body or any other thing that would make him ceremonially unclean. He was to be holy, separated, fully dedicated to God. But ordinarily his vow was for a limited period of time, such as a few weeks or months. And he himself made the vow to become a Nazirite.

Hannah's son would be different. His dedication to God would be for life. It would not be a matter of choice for him. He would be dedicated before he would be old enough to decide for himself. He was to be the Lord's unique possession.

Many people today dedicate their children to God in infancy. But Hannah dedicated Samuel before his birth—even before his conception. What tremendous faith she displayed!

It is interesting to note that Hannah assumed the responsibility for her son's spiritual welfare. Modern parents often are content to wait and let their children decide for themselves at an older age. They do not urge them or encourage them to accept the claims of Christ personally. What a tragic mistake! The worst thing that we can do to our children is give them the impression that surrender to the Lord is optional.

HER PAYMENT

The third event in Hannah's life that shows us her greatness as a mother is her *payment*. It was a sacrifice for Hannah to pray to the Lord. Prayer always involves sacrifice. It was a greater sacrifice for her to promise her son. But the greatest sacrifice was when it came time to pay her vow.

Hannah had prayed diligently to the Lord for a son, and God answered her prayer. God listened to Hannah's cry. He seemed to say, "I have found my kind of mother, and now I shall have my kind of man." He took this simple, uneducated, plain woman, and He answered her prayers.

Hannah would be out of place among the wealthy or elite. She was not the kind that is listed in the society pages. But she made the V.I.P. list of heaven, and God honored her with a son.

Hannah had made a promise to God. Within a few short years the time came for her to give Samuel back. During all those years as she nursed him, cared for him, loved him, watched him grow, she never forgot her vow to the Lord, and she never wavered on whether to pay it.

Hannah was made of the stuff of which martyrs are made! I can just see her gathering clothes, assembling all the provisions for the journey. Her heart is both sad and glad. She occasionally looks down at little Samuel and listens to his childish words. She would miss him very much. But he was the Lord's, not hers to keep.

Hannah gave Samuel up at a very young age. First Samuel 1:24 tells us that he went to the Tabernacle to live as soon as he was weaned. From what we know of the culture of that time, Samuel was probably five years old when he left home. Arriving at the house of the Lord, Hannah greeted the attendant and gave him Samuel and his little bundle of clothes. The moment of parting had come. Hannah gave her little boy one last hug and turned around and walked the lonely road homeward.

Her words are an inspiration: "I have lent him to the LORD; as long as he liveth he shall be lent to the LORD (1 Samuel 1:28). And so she paid her vow.

What a beautiful picture is Hannah of a mother yielded to God! She gave her son to the Lord—not to things, not to society, not even to her country. She gave him to God!

Who can know the ways of God? God uses this woman's barrenness, her family conflicts, and her heartaches to drive her to her knees. She sought God's will completely and by faith dedicated her little son to Him. And God used that boy in a great way to benefit the entire nation.

Mothers, is your commitment to God's will like Hannah's? Are you consecrated to the Lord yourself, and are you willing to consecrate your children? Are you willing to dedicate your child to God, knowing that He may take him away from you? Do you seek God's will for your child, knowing that he may be called to serve the Lord on a foreign mission field far away from you? Is your love for the Lord that strong? And is your love for your child that strong? God's will is not always easy, but it is always best.

And mothers, is your life an example of sacrifice and dedication, as was Hannah's? Samuel grew up in the house of Eli, which certainly was no good influence for him. Eli was lazy, lackadaisical, and lenient; and his sons were immoral, ungodly, and crude. But the example of godliness Samuel had seen in his mother in those early years never left him. He grew up to become a wise and good leader for Israel, and a man of God.

Are you that kind of influence for your child?

And children, does your life speak well of the example of

your mother? Augustine, the great church Father and theologian, had a mother that devoted her life to his Christian upbringing and his conversion to Christ. In his early years it appeared that her efforts had failed. Augustine lived carelessly. He flouted moral restraint and actively rebelled against God. But one day he was brought to his senses and remembered his praying mother and the Word of God. He was gloriously converted and became a champion of the faith.

There once was a young lady who ignored the claims of Christ. She laughed at her mother's prayers and turned her back on her mother's God. She seemed to be headed for an eternity without God. There came a day, however, when she was moved to pen these words:

> I grieved my Lord from day to day,
> I scorned His love so full and free.
> And though I wandered far away,
> My mother's prayers have followed me.
>
> I'm coming home, I'm coming home,
> To live my wasted life anew,
> For mother's prayers have followed me,
> Have followed me the whole world through.*

Some of you had Christian mothers who prayed for you. They have prayed for years, but as yet you have not come home. You have refused to give your life to the Lord Jesus Christ. Perhaps your mother has already gone to heaven. She is there waiting for you, my friend. Do you intend to prepare for the final homecoming? Will you receive Christ right now? He knocks, He calls, but you must open your life to Him.

*Lizzie DeArmond, "Mother's Prayers Have Followed Me."
Copyright 1912 by B. D. Ackley (c) Renewed 1940, The Rodeheaver Co. Used by permission.

8

God's Power for Faithful Mothers

Several years ago a very unusual letter came to the office of *Moody Monthly* magazine. It read:

> Dear Magazine Publishers,
>
> If you ever have a Mother of the Year contest, I feel that you should pick my mom.
>
> The reason is because my mom is one mom that really cares about me. My mom disciplines me when I'm bad and is nice to me when I'm good, and she works every day from morning to night, and when she comes home, she's in a good mood, when most mothers aren't.
>
> My mom is one mom that needs something to live about and be proud of. I sure love my mom and I want her to lead a beautiful life; and most of all I want to be proud of her. So, please, could you make her mother of the year? Thank you.
>
> Sincerely, Paul

That is all. There is no street or address. There is not even named a town from where it was sent. But it's just as well because we do not have a Mother of the Year contest. How could we ever choose? In God's eyes as well as in the eyes of their families, many sincere, godly mothers are mothers of the year.

To mothers are entrusted the most precious of God's creation—children. They have the responsibility, shared with the fathers, to train up the children in the way that they should go. To parents more than anyone else is given the opportunity to raise children in the nurture and admonition of the Lord. And the influence of the mother certainly is felt.

Every year for the parents is the year that counts. Next year may be too late. The little lives in your sphere of influence must be nurtured, protected, guided, and pointed to Jesus Christ right now! Today's opportunities may not remain for tomorrow.

But God knows all that. He sees and cares. He is infinitely concerned about mothers and their needs. How do I know? The Bible tells me so. The mothers in the Bible show by their lives that God makes special provision for the special needs of mothers. Let's look at the messages in the lives of several Bible mothers.

Eve—God's Power to Defeat Satan

Eve was the first mother and the mother of the entire race. Motherhood for Eve must have been a frightening thing. No one had ever been a mother before, and she and Adam had just lost everything because of sin. Satan had beguiled Eve, she and Adam had disobeyed God, and all creation had been placed under a curse. Adam and Eve had lost their right to live in the Garden of Eden. They could no longer walk and talk with God, and death for them was a certainty.

But as we look at the life of Eve, we see *God's power to defeat Satan.* Satan had appeared to Eve as a serpent and had tricked her into leading Adam into sin. God had told them that the consequences of disobedience would be death, but they had disobeyed anyway, and God pronounced a curse on them.

78

But with the curse was a promise, and that was the promise of a deliverer. Genesis 3:15 records God's curse on the serpent, Satan. "And I will put enmity between thee and the woman, and between thy seed and her seed; it shall bruise thy head, and thou shalt bruise his heel."

My friend, do you see the importance of those words? Although Eve had been the instrument of Satan in the human downfall, she would have a part with God in the redemption of the human race. Her motherhood would ultimately mean Satan's defeat. A child born to her would become the deliverer who would crush the head of the serpent and defeat Satan.

Eve realized that. Perhaps that is why she named her first son "Cain," or "gotten one," adding, "I have gotten a man from the LORD." It seemed that she thought he was the promised deliverer. Of course, we know that God's promise was not to be fulfilled directly through Eve but through one of Eve's descendants, Mary of Nazareth. Her Son, Jesus, truly crushed the head of Satan, completely defeating him, and, as Colossians 2:15 tells us, openly triumphing over him in His own death and resurrection.

But Eve was a vital link in the line that at last led to Jesus Christ our Savior. Her motherhood demonstrates God's power to defeat Satan. God uses people. And for each person He sends into the world, He needs a mother. And He needs mothers that are godly.

Think of how God defeated Satan's working in Eve. He dealt with her *sin*. Genesis 3:21 tells us that the Lord God made clothing of animal skins for Adam and Eve. It is my belief that God's purpose in that was only partly to give Adam and Eve a covering for their nakedness. They had made their own clothing by sewing together some large leaves (verse 7). But in using animal skins, God had to slay some animals. Adam and Eve surely witnessed that event, probably the first time blood was shed for any purpose.

Hebrews 9:22 tells us that without shedding of blood there is no remission of sin. The shedding of blood was God's first lesson to man in the doctrine of atonement. Those animal skins made a covering for Adam and Eve, but the deaths of the animals by the shedding of blood made a covering for their sins. And that is what atonement is—a covering for sins.

But God dealt also with her *sorrow.* And her sorrow was great. She surely had sorrow over her sin and loss of fellowship with God. And God Himself had promised her sorrow in childbearing. But He also had, through childbearing, given her a reason for hope. A redeemer was coming. The redeemer that was to come, the Lord Jesus Christ, did more than just cover sin—He took it away. So God's provision dealt with their sin.

Satan had tried to destroy mankind, but instead he was destroyed himself. And Eve's life stands as a testimony to the power of God to defeat Satan.

JOCHEBED—GOD'S POWER TO OVERRULE CIRCUMSTANCES

Look now at the life of another mother. Jochebed, the mother of Moses, shows us *God's power to overrule circumstances.* Like Eve, Jochebed became a mother at a time of great sorrow. The king of Egypt, where Jochebed lived, had issued an order to the Egyptian midwives that when an Israelite boy was born, he should be killed (Exodus 1:16). It was the first major persecution of the Jewish people.

Jochebed, an Israelite woman, feared God, and she trusted God. When a son was born to her, she hid him for three months (Exodus 2:2). And when she was no longer able to hide him, she put him in the river among some weeds and sent his sister to watch to see what God would do. Hebrews 11:23 gives us some wonderful insight into what was in Jochebed's heart as she hid her son at the river.

First, it was an act of faith. Jochebed was confident that

God who was able to overcome Satan also was able to overrule circumstances. Hebrews 11 tells us that she acted in faith.

Second, notice that she was not afraid of the king's commandment. For three months as she did her best to conceal the existence of her little son, she was not afraid. Her faith in God gave her confidence. She worshiped a God who was able to overcome circumstances, and the king's commandment was nothing compared to God's power.

Look how God overruled the negative circumstances for Jochebed. First, Moses lived. Despite the king's order and his all-out campaign to destroy the Israelite boys, Jochebed was able to keep her son.

Also, Moses not only lived, but he lived in luxury as well. God had His hand on this little baby, and even though he was marked for death by Pharaoh, he lived. And what is more, he lived in Pharaoh's own household! Exodus 2:5-6 tells us that Pharaoh's own daughter found the baby Moses and took him home to care for him.

That is the way God works. Man can shake his fist in defiance of God; he can attempt to thwart God's purposes; and he can even take stringent measures to see to it that he has his way instead of God's. But in the end, God always overrules the circumstances, and Pharaoh ends up with the one he was so determined to kill living in his own household.

Have you considered what it meant to Moses to be raised in Pharaoh's house? He had access to all the finest things in Egypt. He had the finest education that could be had. He walked among prime ministers and governors. And his exposure to all that gave him the best training for leadership that the world could offer.

But that is not all God did to overrule the circumstances. He made it possible for Jochebed to stay with her son! God rewarded her faith by sovereignly ordaining that when

Pharaoh's daughter sought a nurse for the boy, Jochebed was the one that was chosen. What a wonderful God we have who can overrule every circumstance!

BATHSHEBA—GOD'S POWER TO CHANGE A LIFE

Finally, look with me at the life of yet another mother: Bathsheba, the mother of Solomon. You know the sordid story of Bathsheba and David's sin with her. It all began with a look. David lusted after Bathsheba, committed adultery with her, had her husband killed, and then married her. The record of that sin is one of the saddest chapters in all the Bible. But the whole story of Bathsheba is the story of *God's power to change a life.*

David and Bathsheba had an illegitimate child, who died soon after he was born. Second Samuel 12:24 tells us that after the death of that child, Bathsheba bore to David another child, whom they named Solomon. And the Scripture adds these meaningful words: "and the LORD loved him."

Why does the Scripture make it a point to say that the Lord loved Solomon? It is the Holy Spirit's way of letting us know that God's forgiveness of David and Bathsheba was complete. God had blotted out their sin, and He would remember it no more. This new child born out of their union was to have the blessing and love of God in a special way.

And God did bless Solomon. Out of all David's sons, it was Solomon who was chosen to occupy the throne in Israel after him. He was blessed with wisdom by the Lord, and he was used of the Lord to write three books of Scripture. One of those was the book of Proverbs, most of which was penned by Solomon. Look at the last chapter of that book.

Proverbs 31 begins, "The words of king Lemuel, the prophecy that his mother taught him." Many Bible students believe that Lemuel was actually Solomon, and that

"Lemuel" was his mother's pet name for him. The chapter is a collection of the advice his mother gave to him. She advises him on matters of morality, judgment, and the proper behavior of kings.

Where did Bathsheba get such wisdom? How did one who sinned so outrageously have the insight and understanding to advise the king on matters of morality? I believe that God had transformed her life. She was not the same weak-willed woman that had committed adultery with David.

Look especially at the final twenty-two verses of Proverbs 31. Beginning with verse 10 he describes the virtuous woman. Do you think Solomon would have taken seriously his mother's advice about women if she herself did not exemplify those qualities? I feel that the description in Proverbs 31 is a description of Bathsheba, and it is a wonderful demonstration of God's power to change a life.

The relationship that began as adultery ended with God's approval and blessing. God was able to take man's sin and work it unto His own glory. And because David and Bathsheba sincerely repented of their sin, He was able to transform two lives for His glory.

Mothers, can you identify with these Bible mothers? Perhaps you see Satan working hard to influence and corrupt your children. Then look at Eve, and see God's power to defeat Satan. Or perhaps you can see the circumstances of life threatening your family with problems. Then remember Jochebed, and see God's power to overcome circumstances. Maybe you feel inadequate as a mother. Perhaps your faith, or your relationship to the Lord are not what they ought to be. Or maybe some sin from your past life haunts you with feelings of guilt. Then look at Bathsheba, and take note of God's power to change a life.

God is omnipotent. His power can defeat Satan, overcome circumstances, and change lives. There is nothing that can come in the way of your responsibilities as a parent that God's power cannot overcome. The key is faith.

Eve displayed faith when she allowed God to provide clothing and a sacrifice for her. She could have persisted in the way she had begun, sewing flimsy clothing out of fig leaves for herself. That clothing was adequate as a covering, at least for a while. But it could not do anything for her sin, and it lacked the permanence that God's provision of animal skins gave. It represented man's good works, which just never are good enough.

But Eve responded to God in faith. She put aside her own works and accepted God's clothing of righteousness. That was an act of faith.

Jochebed displayed faith when she hid her son. As we have seen, she was not afraid of Pharaoh's power. She acted in faith, and God responded by giving her more than she could have asked for or wished for.

Bathsheba, too, showed faith. In coming to God for forgiveness, she was coming in faith. By faith was the only way she could come. She could not offer to do anything to atone for her sin, because it is "not by works of righteousness which we have done, but according to his mercy he saved us" (Titus 3:5). No person can earn forgiveness from sin by good works. It must be accepted by faith.

And God honored Bathsheba's faith. She is one of three women listed in Matthew's genealogy of our Lord (Matthew 1:6). Through David and Bathsheba came the line that was to bring the Messiah, God's anointed Deliverer, the Lord Jesus Christ.

Mother, will you respond to God in faith? Will you by faith receive the power you need to fulfill your responsibilities as a mother?

Children and fathers, the invitation is open to you, too. God will supply your needs. And you must trust Him for it—you cannot work for it. "For by grace are ye saved through faith; and that not of yourselves: it is the gift of God: not of works, lest any man should boast" (Ephesians 2:8-9). The Lord is calling you today. "My calling is a holy one. Trust me and do not be afraid."

9

What It Takes to Be a Good Father

Some people say that any man can be a father. It's a job, they say, that takes very little talent. The facts, however, show that the rate of failure at fatherhood is higher than in any other occupation. Being a father is actually a colossal job that most people underestimate.

What does it take to be an adequate father? How do you measure up? Is it true that being a father is the most important job a man can have? I believe so.

And I believe that being a father is not a part-time job. The man that would be a true father, a father that does his job well and fulfills his responsibilities, must work at it full time. And there are not many full-time fathers these days.

In a recent book, Dr. Charlie Shedd describes an interesting experience.[1] He was on board a plane jetting to Los Angeles. In the seat beside him sat a well-dressed, young-looking man. He was absorbed in a magazine article on teenagers and the current drug problem. There were pictures, too, of what drugs can do to people.

When he finished the article, the young man closed the magazine and stared into space. Apparently forgetting those around him, he half-spoke, half-whispered what seemed to be a prayer.

"Oh, God—I wonder why! I suppose nobody knows."

And then he added quickly, "But if a father can make the difference, I sure want to make the difference!"

Dr. Shedd could not pass by the young man's concern. He learned that the young man so burdened about his role as a father was a successful businessman—a salesman for a well-known firm. He had a wife and three fine children. Success in business seemed written in his future. But there was nothing higher on his agenda for the years ahead than to be an effective father—a father that would "make the difference."

The Bible makes it clear that the ideal pattern for every home and family is built on a godly father. The father is the dominant figure in the family, and his role is vital. The Bible repeatedly implies that to be without a father is the greatest of afflictions for a family. God Himself is moved to pity the fatherless. Hosea says, "In thee the fatherless findeth mercy" (Hosea 14:3). The psalmist wrote, "He relieveth the fatherless and widow" (Psalm 146:9).

But even worse than a home without a father is a home in which the father fails to fulfill his role. And there are many these days. Maybe they are too busy. Maybe they are careless. Or maybe they do not see the full dimensions of a father's task. Whatever the reason, one of our greatest needs today is for fathers to fill their roles and do it full time.

Looking at God's Word, I see three main needs in a family that the father has a duty to give his full time to supply.

PROVISION FOR THE FAMILY

The first need of every family, and probably the most obvious, is the material need. The full-time father's duty is to supply *provision for the family.*

Not very many fathers fail here. We may not give them all they would like, but we take pride in giving them all we are able. The Bible says that is the way it should be. First

Timothy 5:8 says, "But if any provide not for his own, and specially for those of his own house, he hath denied the faith, and is worse than an infidel."

Providing is a great privilege for the parent. Paul writes, "For the children ought not to lay up for the parents, but the parents for the children" (2 Corinthians 12:14).

A man who does not do his best to provide the material needs of his family commits a great sin. In the words of the Bible, he is worse than an unbeliever. No greater charge could be hurled at anyone.

But perhaps the greater danger for most of us today is that we sometimes provide beyond our real needs. A father can set his family's standards of material wants too high. He can lead his children to want and expect too much by overstressing the importance of money. The wise father will not infect his family with the love of money, which Paul says brings many sorrows. His counsel to Timothy in 1 Timothy 6:8 is, "Having food and raiment let us be therewith content."

But the father's duty to supply provision for the family does not stop with material needs. More important, but often completely forgotten, are such spiritual and emotional needs as love, training, a positive example, encouragement, and spiritual leadership.

The father is the spiritual leader of the family—or he should be. In 1 Timothy and Titus, Paul gives lists of qualifications for elders and deacons—the men who have spiritual authority over the church. And each time, the qualification that heads the list is the requirement that he be a good spiritual leader in his own family.

Consider the word *father*. There is no more important word in any language. God even uses the word to describe Himself and His relationship to His people. The word speaks of life itself, of love and patience, of discipline and strength and refuge. All those are things God provides for

89

us—and we must provide them for our earthly children.

Fathers, your responsibility to be a spiritual leader to your family cannot be overstated. You stand symbolically in the same position over your family that God stands in over His people. You actually represent God to your family! You have given your children life, and now you must give them what they need for spiritual growth.

Do you give your children the training they need in the Word of God? If you don't, who will? No one else has the opportunities or the influence that you have in the spiritual training of your children, and you must fulfill your duties.

Training in righteousness includes not only the whats and the hows of life, but the whys as well. The Bible is your textbook, and you can teach it only as well as you can exemplify it in your life.

You must teach your children to respond to authority. The boy or girl who has learned to love and obey his parents has taken the first step toward obeying and trusting God. God's Word makes it clear that discipline is vital. "Correct thy son, and he shall give thee rest," says Proverbs 29:17. "Yea, he shall give delight unto thy soul."

It is easy to be a permissive father, but it is costly beyond words. Proverbs again reminds us, "He that spareth his rod hateth his son: but he that loveth him chasteneth him" (Proverbs 13:24).

You also must provide love for your children. One of the basic human needs is love. Love assures your children that they really matter. Your love is an anchor of security that tells them they are really important to you, no matter what may happen.

Give your children the kind of love God shows to His children. Beware of giving the kind of love that loves only when they are pleasing you. God's love is not the kind of love that asks something in return. It is a love that loves even when we are undeserving. But God's love also firmly and lovingly corrects and rebukes.

Fathers, do you love your children? And do you spend time with them? You may think you have good reasons for making your business a priority over your children, but God can see through the flimsiness of them—and so can your children. There is no substitute for spending time with them, for being interested in their interests. They do not need the things you can buy them half as much as they need you. Your work is not more important than your children. And that goes for pastors and others in Christian work.

Protection for the Family

A second need that every father has a duty to supply is *protection for the family.* Again, the father has the same role over his family that God has over His people. God protects and nurtures his children, and every father has that same responsibility.

Few fathers fail to provide physical protection for their families. It would be hard to find a father who, if someone came into his house threatening his children with physical harm, would not fight to the death to protect his family. That sense of duty seems to be engraved in our very nature. We look with utter contempt on a man who does not provide for his family's material needs, but we would respond in anger and disgust to a man who would not protect his family from physical harm.

And yet physical dangers are not the only things that threaten our families and children today. The spiritual dangers that confront our modern homes are overwhelming. Fathers, do you seek to provide spiritual protection for your family?

How can you protect your family spiritually? First, you must set an example of spiritual strength and stability. If Satan can get a foothold in your life, he will have a foothold in your family. Be yielded to the Lord. "Resist the devil, and he will flee from you" (James 4:7). Arm yourself with the spiritual armor of God listed in Ephesians 6. Is your breastplate on right? More important, do you have the right helmet? Are you familiar with your offensive weapon, the Word of God? If there is one weak point in your armor, you and your family are unnecessarily exposed. Protect your family!

How else can you protect your family? Be sure that they are not exposed to dangerous teaching. Be sure that the church you go to teaches and believes the Word of God. Be alert to what comes into your home via the television. And train your children in the truth.

PRAYER FOR THE FAMILY

Finally, every father has a duty to supply *prayer for the family*. Are you praying for your children? How much that prayer can mean!

Job was a praying father. Job 1:5 tells us that Job made it a habit to pray for each of his children. What a great thing it is to have a praying father!

David prayed for Solomon, and his prayer launched him into the pinnacle reign of the Old Testament. Under Solomon's kingship, the nation of Israel gained heights of glory and wealth never again attained. It began with a father's prayer.

Fathers, one of the greatest sins you can commit against your children is the sin of prayerlessness. God has committed your children to you, and part of your responsibility is to pray for them. You are to punish them when they do wrong and praise them when they do right, but pray for them at all times.

The time you spend in prayer for your family is rich. It benefits you as you draw nearer to the Lord with your heart's burdens. And it benefits your family as God answers your prayers and you see their growth.

Paul was a father. Not a physical father but a spiritual

one. All the churches he had begun, all the people he had won to the Lord, were his special children. Look through his epistles and see how many times he assures his spiritual children that he does not cease to pray for them. He understood that one of the responsibilities inherent in spiritual leadership is the duty to pray for those under that leadership. And he set a good example for all fathers to follow.

Yes, being a father is a full-time occupation. And its rewards can be rich. John wrote about his spiritual children, "I havs no greater joy than to hear that my children walk in truth" (3 John 4).

Sometimes there are effects of our influence that we may never know. Brooks Adams kept a diary from his boyhood. One special day when he was eight years old he wrote in his diary, "Went fishing with my father; the most glorious day of my life." Throughout the next forty years of his life, he never forgot that day he went fishing with his father; he made repeated references to it in his diary, commenting on the influence that day had had on his life.

Brooks' father was an important man; he was Charles Francis Adams, the United States' ambassador to Great Britain under the Lincoln administration. Interestingly, he too made a note in his diary about the fishing trip. He wrote simply, "Went fishing with my son; a day wasted."

Of course, the day was not wasted; its value may well have proved to make it one of the most wellspent days in his life. No one can measure the influence of a man on his children, and that is all the more reason to take the job and its responsibilities seriously.

Fathers, are you providing for your children? Are you really giving them all that they need? Are you protecting them? And are you praying for them? May God help you to be a full-time father.

1. Charlie Shedd, *Smart Dads I Know* (New York: Sheed and Ward, 1975), pp. ix-x.

10

Filling a Father's Shoes

If you were asked to name the world's hardest job, what would you say it is? Serving as president of the United States? Heading up the United Nations? Serving Jesus Christ somewhere as a missionary or pastor?

Each of those choices could be defended. But I believe that an even harder job than any of those is being a good parent. And today I'm thinking especially of the work of the father. I want to tell you why a father's job tops nearly every other. And if you are a father, I want to suggest some insight into what your job is and how you can do it better.

In a new book, *The Effective Father,* Gordon MacDonald describes an exciting moment while canoeing with his son in a treacherous stretch of rapids. "The river was a boiling white," he recalls, "running furiously, smashing around and over rocks, here and there climbing to gunwale-high waves. Our "survival" depended upon being able to pick a route back and forth across the river that would avoid . . . tipping over and losing everything—especially our pride as great wilderness explorers.

"Then it happened! A water-soaked tree . . . caught the shoekeel of our Grumman canoe. . . . In an instant we were upside down in freezing water." Apparently the incident had a happy ending. Both canoeists emerged unhurt and in due time were afloat again, a little more careful and a little wiser. MacDonald saw the experience as an illustration of the perils the average father faces most of the time. A father must make decisions—right decisions—and he dare not make them in a state of confusion or panic or bewilderment. A father, like a person steering a canoe, must always be ahead of the upcoming situation. The effective father, says MacDonald, must look downriver in the life of his family, preparing to make good decisions. His job is to keep the family dry.[1]

You can be a good father, but faith and good intentions are not enough. Even a godly man can be a failure as a father. Samuel, David, and Aaron are some men in the Bible who show that that is true.

The Bible, in fact, tells of many who failed in their task as fathers. Isaac was partial to Esau. You cannot read of his home life without sensing that he failed in raising his sons.

Jacob in turn was a failure. Genesis 34 tells of a crisis in his family in which he failed to act at all. As a result, an entire community perished.

Eli failed to guide his sons into a walk with God, and his house came tumbling down around his ears.

Solomon's son was weak and foolish, a living reminder that even this wisest of men was a failure as a father.

The question of the failure of so many fathers in the Bible is a troubling one. Why did they fail? And how can we fathers today avoid the same kind of failure? Consider with me three important questions about fatherhood.

WHAT IS A FATHER?

The first question is, *What is a father?* A father is a parent, a partner in transmitting human life. He is a protector and a provider. He also is a teacher sharing knowledge and instruction about living in our world.

Being an effective father is a staggering responsibility. It is one thing to guide your own footsteps; it is quite another to guide someone else's.

Many fail as fathers simply because they underestimate their task. They think that if they can pay their bills and make everyday decisions, the long-range plan will come out all right. But often—very often—it simply does not work that way, and the rate of failure among the fathers may well be higher than that of any other occupation.

When someone is needed to fill a place in a business organization, the company makes out a job description. A job description for a father could read something like this:

> The father must be a man of vision, strength, and character, capable of leading an in-service training organization that will in time reproduce parents like himself. He must carry on his training at all age levels. He must be able to cooperate effectively with the helpmate of his choice, give advice and counsel as needed, and provide spiritual help and leadership. He must care for his own personal problems, prepare his own budgets, and maintain good public relations. He must be a qualified service and repair man. He must be willing to do whatever is needed, twenty-four hours a day, 365 days a year.

> Finally, he must provide his own salary as well as the financial needs of the entire organization.

Now that's a job description! But it only begins to spell out the real responsibilities of an effective father. Surely no other calling is as demanding. A father must transmit to his children God's basic revelation—that we are God's creatures, accountable to Him in all we are and do. He is the source of right and justice in the home. he must be an arbiter, a leader, a provider, a teacher, and a counselor.

Examine the role of the father closely, and you begin to see a tiny likeness to God's own role with reference to the human race. As God in His infinite wisdom loves and rules and provides for all creation, so the human father is to nourish, protect, and guide his little family. David clearly perceived that likeness when he wrote Psalm 103. Verse 13 of that psalm says, "Like as a father pitieth his children, so the LORD pitieth them that fear him."

The Lord Jesus spoke of God as "your heavenly Father."

The point, of course, is not that father has rights and powers superior to those in his family, although in many ways he does. But the real truth is that he must use his position to minister to his family's needs. He is their protector and provider. They are guarded by his love.

As the one in authority over your family, as the one responsible to provide for them and protect them, you are God's representative to them. That, of course, is not to say that God does not deal directly with them—He does. But in many ways, God deals with those in your family through you—through your authority, through your example, and through your leadership. Thus the child who has a faithful, godly father learns what God Himself is like as he sees the father in the home. He first learns the principles of love and faith and obedience to God within the context of the family circle.

Your children will base their concept of God on what they see in you. Studies show that those who have had fathers who were irresponsible or unfaithful to their duties in the family often have a great deal of difficulty trusting God. They tend to think of God in the context of their father's examples, and as a result, their perception of God is marred.

On the other hand, those who have known loving, faithful, concerned earthly fathers tend to find it easier to develop and maintain a close relationship with the heavenly Father.

Put another way, what I am saying is that you should develop the kind of relationship with your children that you wish them to have with God.

A second question we want to examine is, *Why is a father?* Why does a family need a father? What is the father to do? Of course this is a basic issue. We have already listed some of the duties of a father, and if time allowed we could make an even more extensive list. But I want to look closely at three basic functions that encompass all the duties of a father.

The family without a father faces a very grave hardship. So important to the family is the father that the Word of God regards the lack of the father as a great calamity. In such a situation, however, God makes special provision for the family; He says that He Himself will step into the breach to protect and meet the need. "Thou art the helper of the fatherless," says Psalm 10:14. And Psalm 146:9 declares: "The LORD preserveth the strangers; he relieveth the fatherless and widow."

Why is the father so vital? What functions are there that he must perform that no one else can perform? First, he is to steer or *guide his family.*

Biblically, the family is not designed to be a loose or headless organization. God is a God of order. Ephesians 5:23 says, "The husband is the head of the wife, even as Christ is the head of the church: and he is the saviour of the body." Not only is the father the head of the wife, but he is the head of the family in its entirety as well.

The family is not a democracy. Its authority is vested in a person, and that person is the father. And his authority is derived from God, who is the beginning of all authority.

But with his authority goes a great amount of responsibility. In Ephesians 5, as well as in every other passage that speaks of the father's authority, it is clearly taught that husbands and fathers are not to rule for personal advantage, but for the well-being of the family.

The key word is *responsibility.* As a father, when you view your position, you are to see your responsibility, not your authority. No father who is worth his salt will throw his weight around or demand personal homage. He is there to serve, and his motivating power is the love of Jesus Christ. He recognizes that his position makes him a minister to his family, not one to be ministered to by them. He is there not to demand but to deliver. He is the Lord's representative.

Jesus taught that same truth, and He applied it to every position of authority. Not only that, He exemplified it in His own life. Matthew 20:26-28 says, "But it shall not be so among you: but whosoever will be great among you . . . let him be your servant: Even as the Son of man came not to be ministered unto, but to minister, and to give his life a ransom for many."

Another basic function of a father is to shape or *mold his family* through teaching. He does not do all the teaching, of course—the mother may do much of it—but the father is to oversee all the training that his children receive. He must see that they get the teaching that they need, and he must see that the teaching that they get is the right kind.

That involves many things—personal skills both major and minor, the training received at school, and fun and practical things like sports and hobbies. A father teaches attitudes as well. He builds in his children respect for authority and law, reference for God, a good attitude toward work, respect for human life, concern for one another, and a sense of responsibility.

A father is shaping the lives around him for the complexities of daily living in our confusing world. He should teach love for God and faith in Christ. He must bring his children to the Bible, teach them what it says, what it means for them, how to apply it in daily life, and how to study it for themselves. Remember that, as the Bible often says, the fear of the Lord is the beginning of wisdom.

Fathers, it is your responsibility, and a very large one, to monitor closely the things your children are learning at school. You are seriously damaging your child if you are allowing him to be taught at school values that contradict the values he is taught at home, especially if you let that teaching go unchallenged. If at all possible, you should send your child to a school whose teaching you can endorse. If your child receives six hours of humanistic indoctrination each day at school, it will almost certainly make an impression on him.

Of course, it may not be possible to send your child to a school where biblical values are taught. There may be no such school in your area. If that is the case, your job in teaching your child is even more important. You must be absolutely familiar with the things your child is taught in school, and you must know sound, reasonable, and biblical responses to those things he will learn that are not right. Remember, what he learns is your responsibility. God holds you accountable.

A third basic duty of the father is to *seek God's blessing for his family.* He must pray.

Father, you are the priest of the home. You are the spiritual leader. If you do not pray for your family, who will?

Possibly the cause of more friction in family relationships, the cause of more failure in the home, and the cause of more defeat in the family is the prayerlessness of our parents.

We have examined the overwhelming responsibilities of the father. How can any father approach his duties without first approaching God in prayer? Listen, fathers, we cannot do our job alone. We dare not leave God out of our families. We cannot afford the sin of prayerlessness.

How Is a Father?

A final question about fatherhood we need to ask is, *How is a father?* You may ask, How can any man, given his natural failings as a human being, ever hope to succeed in the massive job of being a father? I can give you the answer in one sentence:

You will have to be like God!

That, you may say, is not an easy answer. And you are right. There is very little about fatherhood that is easy. But in saying that you must be like God, I am not saying anything that puts success in fatherhood out of your reach. You *can* be like God!

I am not saying that you can be perfect and sinless, of course. And I am not saying that you can be all-powerful or all-knowing. But I am saying that you can, and you must, have all the characteristics of God working in your life. You will have to be just, loving, wise, patient, merciful, self-giving, tender, and a lot of other things. And God can enable you to be that kind of father.

You remember that I said that you are God's representative to your family. God does not ask you to represent Him without giving you the wherewithal to do it. But you must let Him do it for you and not try to transform yourself.

The first step is to receive Christ as your Savior. Let God reshape your life through the salvation that is in Christ. You need *a new birth*. Jesus said to Nicodemus, "Except a man be born again, he cannot see the kingdom of God" (John 3:3). Do not try to slip beyond this point, for it will never work. You must know Christ before you can have His blessings for your family.

Paul wrote, "If any man be in Christ, he is a new creature: old things are passed away; behold, all things are become new" (2 Corinthians 5:17). He will make you a new creation, and only He can do it.

Once you have made that initial step, you will need *communication with the Lord* every day. I have already mentioned the importance of prayer for your family. But now I am talking about prayer for your own personal spiritual needs. And I am talking about reading God's Word daily to get His guidance and wisdom and understanding. You'll need renewal every day.

Make it your business, and one of your priorities, to get alone with God each day and read His Word and pray. It is sheer folly to attempt to undertake the huge task of parenthood without proper daily preparation.

Finally, you'll need *commitment to the task*. Ask God to make you a dedicated father. Make it your unswerving purpose to honor God in the way you lead your family.

Are you in a good church that believes and teaches the Bible and honors the Lord Jesus? If not, that should be one of the first tasks you dedicate yourself to.

Are you a committed father? Do you represent God well to your family? The shoes of a father are big shoes to fill. Won't you today trust God for the wisdom, power, direction, and skill that you must have to fill those shoes? Or are your needs more basic? Do you need to yield to the Lord and accept Christ as your Savior? You can do it right now.

Fathers, our is a huge responsibility, and we cannot wait to come to terms with it. Make your surrender to the Lord complete today.

1. Gordon MacDonald, *The Effective Father* (Wheaton, Ill.: Tyndale, 1977), pp. 139-40.

11

Guidelines for a Christian Marriage

Recently I received a letter from a California housewife in which she described her troubled marriage. "Our home," she wrote, "is in total uproar. My husband and I are fighting constantly. I am a nervous wreck and unable to sleep at night. I cannot go on like this."

Unfortunately those words are echoed in millions of homes around the world. Many marriages today are in trouble. In fact, modern marriage is deeply in trouble.

Almost forty years ago, sociologist Pitirim Sorokin predicted, "Divorces . . . will increase until any profound difference between socially sanctioned marriages and illicit sex-relationship disappears. . . . The main sociocultural functions of the family will further decrease until the family becomes a mere incidental cohabitation of male and female, while the home will become an overnight parking place."[1]

Although those words have yet to be fully realized, it is not too difficult to see the very real possibility of their complete fulfillment in the immediate future. There is no mistake—marriage is in trouble!

Today, nearly one in every four marriages ends in divorce before the tenth anniversary. In fact, in some densely populated areas of the country, the divorce rate is as high as 70 percent.

In addition to the soaring divorce rates, attitudes about the family are changing. As far back as 1970, a majority of teenagers and adults were becoming disillusioned with the importance of the family. A Harris survey in that year indicated that a majority of persons questioned believed that the family had declined in importance in the previous ten years. That opinion was expressed by 52 percent of the teenagers and 64 percent of the adults surveyed.

In a book entitled *The Death of the Family,* radical sociologist David Cooper calls for the abolition of the family.[2] Modern tensions and demands on individuals, he claimed, have rendered the family unworkable.

And many Americans are experimenting with alternate life-styles. Communal living, homosexual marriages, short-term marriages, live-in agreements, and other alternatives to marriage that were socially unacceptable only a few years ago are now rapidly gaining in acceptance and popularity. As the family deteriorates, more and more young people experiment with such harmful and unscriptural life-styles. And our society turns its back on marriage and the family in what seems to be an alarmingly widespread movement.

Psychiatrist Dr. Thomas P. Malone predicts that, before long, marriage will universally be on a short-term, contract basis. An article that appeared several years ago in *Ladies' Home Journal* quoted Dr. Malone: "A lot of people nowadays . . . think it is idiotic to put two people together at the age of twenty and expect them to be happy for fifty years. What we may shortly be talking about is a three year contract."[3] Dr. Malone concludes by predicting that we will soon be seeing a greater acceptance of trial marriages.

And his predictions seem to be taking shape. Already in several state legislatures, bills have been introduced that would put marriage on a contractural basis. All that would be needed to dissolve the marriage would be the mutual consent of the two partners.

In the midst of all these frightening developments, what can the Christian do? Are there any biblical guidelines for Christian marriage? How can a Christian young couple avoid marital problems that lead to divorce? Even a casual examination of the Bible reveals that it has many things to say concerning marriage. I would like to sum up all those things in three guidelines for a Christian marriage.

MARRIAGE IS A PERMANENT RELATIONSHIP

First of all, and foundational to a biblical understanding of marriage, is the truth that *marriage is a permanent relationship.* In Mark 10:6-7, Jesus said, "From the beginning of the creation God made them male and female. For this cause shall a man leave his father and mother, and cleave to his wife." And then in verse nine we read, "What therefore God hath joined together, let not man put asunder."

Christian couple, your marriage is a sacred union, a work of God, and to dissolve that union is to fall short of what God wants. Many young couples today enter into the marriage relationship with the idea that if it doesn't work out, they can get a divorce. A marriage built on that kind of attitude is doomed before it even begins.

The key to understanding the permanence of marriage is to realize that God planned for man and woman to be together. Marriage is a provision of God for man. He has ordained it, and He designed it to be permanent. In the Garden of Eden, God said that it was not good for man to be alone, and He designed a helper for him. God did not work out a trial marriage for Adam. He did not arrange a short-term contract. When God brought Adam and Eve together, they were to be one flesh forever.

Even in today's wedding vows something about the permanence of marriage is included. Usually both the husband and the wife pledge their love to one another "for

107

better or for worse, for richer or for poorer, in joy and in sorrow, in sickness and in health, *as long as we both shall live.*" That is God's plan, and you dare not say those vows without heartfelt meaning.

If you are planning a marriage, my advice is that you frankly discuss with your future mate the seriousness of the plans you are making. Have an understanding that marriage is permanent, and divorce is never an option for you. If you feel that that is too confining, then you had better not get married.

And if you are already married and have never confronted this issue, I suggest that you get together with your spouse and talk it over. Agree to abide by your sacred vows and keep your marriage permanent. Covenant together never to discuss divorce as a possible solution to your problems. God's will for you is that you remain married.

MARRIAGE IS A HARMONIOUS PARTNERSHIP

A second biblical guideline is that *marriage is a harmonious partnership.* The Bible speaks of the union of the husband and wife as harmonious. Jesus said, "And they twain shall be one flesh: so then *they are no more twain,* but one flesh" (Mark 10:8, italics added).

I have never known of a broken marriage where the husband and wife had enjoyed a true partnership that had been harmonious and mutually sacrificial. But God established marriage to be just that, and His Word gives strict guidelines about how to keep harmony in the home.

Did you know that the relationship of the husband and wife is similar to the relationship of Christ and the church? In his letter to the Ephesians, Paul writes, "The husband is the head of the wife, even as Christ is the head of the church" (Ephesians 5:23). Christ's relationship with the church certainly is a harmonious relationship, isn't it?

Each of the partners in a marriage has a role, and his

understanding that role and fulfilling it is vital to harmony in the marriage. What is the role of the husband? Husbands are to love their wives, "even as Christ loved the church and gave himself for it" (Ephesians 5:25). The husband is to display a *sacrificial love,* the kind of love Christ demonstrated for the church.

What is the role of the wife? "Wives, submit yourselves unto your own husbands, as unto the Lord" (Ephesians 5:22). The wife is to display a *submissive love,* the same kind of love she responds to the Lord with.

I want you to notice something with me. The husband is told to sacrifice for his wife, and the wife is told to submit to her husband. Both duties involve giving, not receiving. Marriage is a giving relationship. The husband is not to demand submission from his wife, and the wife is not to demand sacrifice from her husband. Marriage is not a set of demands for the partner, but a life of service to the partner.

If the husband loves his wife as this passage teaches, he will not think of his wife as a servant to be ordered around. He will see her rather as a partner and friend, someone with whom to share his dreams—someone to give his life for.

And if the woman is submissive to her husband as this passage also teaches, she will not demand his attention, service, and material goods all the time. She will lovingly seek to minister to him.

And so marriage works beautifully as a mutually sacrificial system, each ministering to the other's needs, and asking nothing in return. And this is marriage as God intended it—a harmonious partnership.

Why are there so few marriages that work like that? The reason is selfishness. Most couples today get married for what they can get out of it. People come into marriage looking primarily for companionship, security, gratification of desires, or position. And although all of those things are desirable, they are not the primary function of marriage.

Marriage is sacrifice, giving, ministering, working, and yielding. And the selfish heart has little room for ideas like those.

Today we are faced with the women's rights movement, minority rights movements, and even a widespread children's rights movement. We are conditioned by our society to demand our rights. But such an approach will not work in marriage. Remember, marriage is not a set of demands, but a life of service.

Many today have misread the issues. We are told by some that the biblical standard for women is unfair, that it makes the women inferior to the man. But the issue is not one of superiority and inferiority; it is an issue of the proper position. The wife is not superior or inferior to the husband, and the husband is not superior or inferior to the wife, any more than the head is superior or inferior to the rest of the body. The husband and wife, the Bible says, are like a head and a body. The head cannot function or exist without the body, and the body cannot function or exist without the head. But they have completely different functions.

In the same way, the husband and wife have separate but complementary functions. They cannot function apart from each other, but their roles *are* different. To make that an issue of superiority or inferiority is a terrible error.

The wife that tries to usurp her husband's role as head of the family destroys the marriage. And the husband that would exchange roles with his wife is guilty of abdicating a God-given responsibility. Harmony cannot exist in the marriage where God's plan for marriage is shunned.

Marriage Is a Spiritual Companionship

But there is a truth that is even greater than the truths that marriage is a permanent relationship and a harmonious partnership. And that is the biblical teaching that *marriage is a spiritual companionship.*

110

Christian marriage should be a companionship where each helps the other to grow in Christ. The Bible tells us that in the marriage relationship, the husband and wife become one. It is my conviction that that speaks not only of a physical union, but of a spiritual union as well.

We talked about the issue of inferiority and superiority. If anyone in marriage is superior, it is the Lord Jesus Christ Himself. He is a partner in a biblical Christian marriage. In fact, He is the center of the home, and around Him everything else revolves. In that sense, the home is a reflection of heaven.

How do I know that? In Matthew 18:20, Jesus said, "For where two or three are gathered together in my name, there am I in the midst of them." And that certainly applies to a Christian marriage, entered into in Christ's name.

Christian couple, do you understand the significance of that? Christ's presence is in a special way permanent in your home. Your home is His dwelling place, and He is there to fellowship with you, lead you, and minister to your needs. Do you live in your home in a way that recognizes His presence?

If the marriage relationship is to be a true spiritual companionship, the husband and wife must have a regular time of spiritual devotions. I mean a time of fellowship and prayer and study together in God's Word. It does not have to be a lengthy time, but it is vital that the husband and wife cultivate a spiritual companionship together.

Through the years I have counseled with many troubled families, and inevitably I have found that the homes with the problems are the homes without God's Word. Recently I read of an eighteen-year old boy who was arrested on charges of armed robbery. As he was questioned it was learned that this boy's parents were Christians. His father was a prominent deacon in the church. His mother taught a Sunday school class, and the whole family attended church regularly. When asked why he, a boy from a background like that, got into so much trouble, he replied, "My folks may be active church members, but we certainly don't have much of a Christian home! I never once have seen my parents pray or read the Bible."

What a shame! Is that true in your home, friend?

A Christian marriage demands Christian living. It demands a commitment—a serious commitment—to the Lord and to His will. It demands obedience. And you will discover, I think, that the saying is true—families that pray together stay together.

Yes, we are living in frightening times! Moral attitudes are changing so rapidly that it is impossible to predict the future. The marriage and the home that are not founded on God's Word are on shaky ground! But in a time of moral decay, in a day when it seems there is no certain standard, it is reassuring to know that God's standards are secure. God's Word is true and trustworthy, and it never changes. Not only that, but it works, as well. It is the only solid foundation on which to build our homes and marriages.

The writer of the book of Hebrews said, "Marriage is honourable in all" (Hebrews 13:4). Marriage, my friend, is God's plan and purpose for mankind. Is your marriage what it ought to be—a permanent relationship, a harmonious partnership, and a spiritual companionship? Are you living according to God's plan? Are you building your home on the foundation of God's Word?

If not, why not today let Christ take control? Surrender your life to the Lord Jesus. Let Him be the center of your home from this day forward.

1. Cited by Joan Cook in "Marriage," *Ladies' Home Journal,* September 1971, p. 192.
2. David Cooper, *The Death of the Family* (New York: Pantheon, 1970), p. 63.
3. Joan Cook, "Marriage," p. 197.

12

How to Have a Happy Home

"Our parents never have time for us," said a teenager being interviewed. "They're always too busy."

"Kids are not like they were when I was young," a parent was overheard to say. "Today they are brash, defiant, rebellious, and immoral. What have we come to?"

In this day of failing families, broken homes, teenage crime, open immorality, and drug abuse, one can see a great deal of truth in both the comments of the teenager and those of the parent. And we can indeed wonder what we have come to. Why are things this way? It is my conviction that at the root of most of society's problems is the real problem of families that are failures.

It is not supposed to be like that. The home is to be a happy place, a place of security, a place of fond memories, where we learn as children how to live as adults in our world.

The home was ordained and established by God. It is the first institution He ordained and the building block of all other God-ordained institutions—nations, churches, cities, or races. In the Garden of Eden, God united Adam and Eve in marriage and blessed the first home. Marriage is not merely for convenience or conventionality; it is God's plan for the happiness of all people. It is lifelong, not temporary. It is God-given, not manmade. It is a duet, not a solo. It is a partnership, not a tug of war.

And it is a relationship where two people are either happy or unhappy.

Who determines whether your marriage is happy or unhappy? You do. Not your in-laws, not your friends, not your children, not even your spouse. You alone are the one who has the power to make your marriage either a happy one or a miserable one. And you determine it by the way you respond to tribulation, which is inevitable in any marriage.

And yet, it seems, many people are not willing to sacrifice and yield to assure a successful marriage and a happy home. There are now almost a million divorces each year in the United States. From broken homes often emerge disillusioned young people with warped ideals. They in turn have families that fail, and so on. The collapse of the home is probably the greatest threat to our world future. Unless there is a return to the biblical patterns for marriage, the family, and the home, our entire civilization faces certain extinction.

Do you want to have a happy home? Do you want to have a family that honors God, lives harmoniously, and is successful? God's Word tells you how. And I would like to look at four ingredients in a happy home.

DISCIPLINE

The first is *discipline.* And by that I mean both self-discipline and parental discipline for the children. The chief value of discipline of any kind is orderliness. If your home is not united, if it is disorganized and fragmented, then your home is suffering from a lack of discipline.

First, you are to discipline yourself. How are you at *personal discipline?* Do you leave things lying around the house? Do you leave things undone until later, and then have to do them at the last moment? Are you able to control your appetites? Parent, if you are not disciplined yourself, you will not be able to discipline your children effectively.

But there are more important things in personal discipline than picking up your socks and being ready to go somewhere on time. Those things involve discipline in the practical realm. Discipline is vital in the spiritual realm, too.

Your walk with the Lord requires discipline. Paul wrote to Timothy, "Study to shew thyself approved unto God" (2 Timothy 2:15). That word "study" means "give diligence" or "be disciplined." The word *disciple* comes from the same word as *discipline.* It takes diligence and discipline to walk with the Lord.

Discipline is required if you are to have a regular daily quiet time. Establishing times of regular prayer requires discipline. In fact, almost everything you must do as a Christian requires discipline, including giving, church attendance, Bible study, and witnessing.

Lack of personal discipline in the home can cause conflicts. Duties are left undone, important things are forgotten, bad habits are accrued, all because of a lack of personal discipline. And all those things become sources of conflict in the family.

Parental discipline also is important in the home. By that I mean that the parents should discipline the children. Children should be trained to do right and punished when they do wrong. The book of Proverbs has much to say about proper discipline for a child. Proverbs 13:24 says that strict discipline is proof of a parent's love. "He that spareth his rod hateth his son: but he that loveth him chasteneth him betimes."

Proverbs 19:18 says much the same thing. "Chasten thy son while there is hope, and let not thy soul spare for his crying." And Proverbs 23:13-14 adds, "Withhold not correction from the child: for if thou beatest him with the rod, he shall not die. Thou shalt beat him with the rod, and shalt deliver his soul from hell."

Why is that? Proverbs 22:15 says, "Foolishness is bound in the heart of a child, but the rod of correction shall drive it far from him." A child is born with a sin nature, with an inclination to do wrong, and proper discipline is one way to lead him away from the evil toward the good.

What is the proper way to discipline a child? The Scriptures are quite clear that corporal punishment is the best way. But you must never inflict injury on a child.

Never strike a child in anger. It is important that he understand that his punishment is just that—a punishment, not a vent for your anger. Before you punish the child, talk to him. Make sure he understands what he is being punished for.

And never let your discipline become a weapon to get even with your children. Paul wrote, "Fathers, provoke not your children to anger, lest they be discouraged" (Colossians 3:21). Discipline must always be done in love. And disciplining your children gives you some of the best opportunities you will have to *en*courage them. Don't waste those opportunities.

DEVOTION

A second ingredient in the happy home is *devotion*. I am referring to devotion to each other as well as devotion to the Lord.

Loyalty is one of the sadly lacking elements in our homes today. Children fight with their brothers and sisters; fathers fight with mothers; and parents fight with their children. God did not ordain the family to be that way.

A spirit of devotion, of love and loyalty, should prevail in our families. The family unit is just that—a unit. And if it is to function properly, in unity, there must be a sense of loyalty.

Why has our devotion to one another in our families dissipated? Because we have forgotten how to serve one

116

another. A family, like a church, is primarily giving, not receiving. Harmony cannot exist in an environment where each person is demanding, always asking, forever taking, constantly being ministered unto and never ministering. And yet that is exactly the situation we have in many families today. How can we expect to have happy homes?

Yes, we have forgotten the great truths of submission and yielded rights. Read Philippians 2 to see the Lord's example of submission. He gave up everything for the sake of others. And that is what we must do if we are to know happy homes.

But perhaps more important than devotion to each other is devotion to the Lord. God designed the family to be a spiritual body. Just like the church and the nation of Israel, one of the main functions God designed it for is corporate worship. The family, then, must be devoted to the Lord.

Your family should belong to a church where the Bible is believed and taught, where Christ is honored, and where you can serve the Lord together. And you should be actively involved in the work of the church. You should attend regularly. You should support the church with your gifts, prayers, and service. There is very little that you can do to unify your family as much as active membership in a sound local church will do.

And your family should meet together for fellowship in the Word of God daily. If your family is too busy to do that, you are too busy. Some families do it at mealtimes; others do it before bedtime; and others do it early in the morning. When you do it does not matter as much as the fact that you must do it. You do not have to spend a long time in family devotions. In fact, just a few minutes in the Word of God and prayer will probably be more effective than a longer period of time, especially if you have a wide range of age difference in your family.

And your devotions should include something for

everyone. If you have little children in your family, be sure to explain the Scriptures in a way they can understand. Devotions together should not be boring but an exciting adventure.

What can *you* do to give your family a greater sense of devotion to one another and to the Lord? There is no substitute for honest, heartfelt devotion in the family.

DISCUSSION

A third ingredient in a happy home is *discussion*. Interviewed members of broken homes consistently point to one cause of failure more than any other, and that is a lack of communication. Do you have open lines of communication in your home? Are your children free to come to you with their problems, no matter how trivial they may seem to you, with the confidence that you will listen with understanding and be able to offer good advice? Few parents can honestly answer yes.

In our busy society with its accelerated pace, one institution has suffered more than any other, and that is the home. Parents are too busy for the children, and the children are too busy for each other.

I began this message with a quotation from a teenager who complained that his parents were just too busy. That statement is echoed daily by millions of children throughout our nation. And their parents never seem to hear their pleas. They somehow think it is the other parent that is guilty. But I urge you to examine your own home life objectively. How much quality time do *you* really spend with your children?

I am not talking about the time you sit around watching television together. That seldom provides an opportunity for discussion or communication. And yet the average American family watches four to six hours of television daily. That does not leave much time for communication.

Another obstacle to communication in many homes is the fact that both parents work full time, leaving the children either with a babysitter or alone at home. No wonder the kids feel neglected!

What does God's Word say? That "children are an heritage of the LORD" (Psalm 127:3), and they dare not be neglected! God has given us our children, and they are our greatest responsibility.

Parent, if you do not have time to spend with your children, you had better rearrange your priorities. Perhaps you are involved in too many activities, or perhaps you watch too much television. Or maybe you should even settle for a simpler life-style and not work so many hours. But you must have time to spend with your children, and you must have open communication in your family.

DETERMINATION

A fourth ingredient in a happy home is *determination*. You cannot have a happy home unless you want it so badly that you are willing to make sacrifices for it. You must be determined that your family is going to be harmonious, united, successful, and happy.

Living in a family is a great privilege. The home is a kind of foretaste of heaven, where Christ is the center, and worship, fellowship, and unity revolve around Him.

But living in a family is a great responsibility, too. It is an opportunity to minister, to sacrifice, to serve, and to grow. And growth in the family takes determination.

At the beginning I said that how you respond to tribulation determines whether you will be happy in marriage. That truth can be applied to the wife, husband, child, or any member of the family. Trials are inevitable. Especially in an environment of close relationships like the family. Conflicts between family members will arise. How will you respond to them?

Did you know that every tribulation that comes to you is allowed by God and is an opportunity for growth? That is the teaching of both James and Paul. James wrote, "My brethren, count it all joy when you fall into divers temptations; knowing this, that the trying of your faith worketh patience. But let patience have her perfect work, that ye may be perfect and entire, wanted nothing" (James 1:2-4).

And what is patience's perfect work? Paul wrote, "We glory in tribulations also; knowing that tribulation worketh patience; and patience, experience; and experience, hope: And hope maketh not ashamed; because the love of God is shed abroad in our hearts by the Holy Ghost" (Romans 5:3-5).

The perfect work of patience in us, then, includes such qualities as confidence, assurance, and the overflowing love of God in our hearts. What better provision could there be for a happy home life?

So you must be determined to respond to tribulations in the home in the proper way. Do not demand your rights. Do not render insult for insult, an eye for an eye and a tooth for a tooth. Respond as Christ would, with love and a willingness to suffer—even wrongfully, if need be, to minister to the needs of the other.

Does your home have those four ingredients: discipline, devotion, discussion, and determination? If so there will be no division. There will be no dissension. There will be no destruction. There will be no dissolution. But there will be new direction and a new dimension of happiness and harmony in the home.

Why not yield today to the lordship of Christ and determine in your heart that you will make the necessary sacrifices to assure that your family life will be a happy and prosperous one?

13

Beautiful, Happy Wives
and Mothers

In our last message we looked at the ingredients in a happy, successful, harmonious home. Those vital ingredients were discipline, devotion, discussion, and determination. You may be thinking that there are very few truly happy homes in our country, and unfortunately that seems to be true.

Why is it that a harmonious and unified family is such a scarce commodity? My feeling is that our families have violated God's established order. Husbands and wives have tried exchanging roles, parents have abdicated responsibility, and children have actually taken over the reins in many families. And it is not working.

The divorce rate continues to soar, juvenile delinquency is ballooning to the point that actually more than half of the crimes that are committed are committed by children, families are dissolving, and America is suffering because of it. Our entire society is in turmoil over issues such as abortion, homosexuality, women's rights, and children's rights. And at the heart of all those issues is God's order for the family.

God has established the family, as we have seen, and He has given detailed instructions in His Word concerning the proper order in the family. The husband has the role of leadership, the wife has the role of helper, and the children have the role of trainees in the art of living. The husband is the *leader,* the wife is a *laborer* together with him, and the children are *learners.* And thus the home works harmoniously, as each does his part to sacrifice, give, and minister to the others in the family.

But our society has rejected the Lord's order of the family, and as a result, it is suffering. The only answer to many of the problems and weaknesses of our nation, I am convinced, is a return to God's standard for family living. We can expect no great national renewal until we return to God's Word and put its principles to work again. The source of our strength as a nation always has been the strength of our individual families. We cannot continue to reject God's principles and remain a nation for very long.

I would like to examine closely what God's Word has to say about the Christian wife in a happy home. What is her role, her ministry to the family? What does she need to fulfill that role adequately? How can you, Christian wives, assure that your homes will be happy, successful homes, built on the foundation of the Word of God and operating after His pattern?

I would especially like to examine four words that describe a godly wife and mother.

SUBMISSION

The first of those four words is *submission.* Paul wrote to the Colossians to describe the roles of family members. "Wives," he said in Colossians 3:18, "submit yourselves unto your own husbands, as it is fit in the Lord."

That is not a popular concept in our society today. Some say that it makes the woman inferior to the man, which simply is not true. Others say that it is unfair, asserting that marriage and the family should be a democracy. And still others claim that it is a cultural thing, to be understood in the context of the Colossian culture in the first century and not applied to today.

But the fact remains that the biblical instruction to wives is that they be submissive. Paul says the same thing in Ephesians 5:22, with a different twist, "Wives, submit yourselves unto your own husbands, *as unto the Lord*" (italics added). Paul says here that submission ought to be as unto the Lord. In other words, the wife is to submit to her husband just as she would to God Himself! There is no softening of the language here, either.

Why does God demand submission from the wife? Because it is His plan. It is the order of creation, Paul says in 1 Corinthians 11:8-9. Man was created first, and then woman. In fact, woman was taken from man. And God designed that the woman was to be under the authority of the man. Again in 1 Corinthians 11, Paul says, "But I would have you know, that the head of every man is Christ; and the head of the woman is the man; and the head of Christ is God" (verse 3). He says the same thing in Ephesians 5:23: "For the husband is the head of the wife, even as Christ is the head of the church."

God has established a definite progression of authority through the Lord Jesus to the husband. That means that when God reveals His will to the family, He does it through the father. God will not usurp His own lines of authority and speak to the wife where He has not spoken to the husband. Therefore, the wife is to be submissive to her husband just as she would be to God, because God has ordained the husband's authority.

This is not a question of superiority of either the man or the woman. Both are superior in their respective positions. No one would suggest that a child is in any way inferior to his parents just because he is under their authority. And the wife certainly is not inferior to her husband although she is under his authority.

Some women, because of personality traits, find it more difficult to be submissive than others do. Nevertheless,

God's order for every family is that the wife yield to the authority of her husband.

And there is nothing more beautiful than the submissive wife who conducts herself according to the Word of God. She does not stifle her own personality or creativity; she fulfills it according to God's will. Therefore she is the one who truly attains her fullest potential.

Wife, do you feel that submission to your husband is too confining? Do you chafe under the idea that you must yield to his authority? If so, you need to learn to trust God in a deeper way. There is no substitute or alternative to His plan for your family, and you must learn to submit to God as well as to your husband.

SERVICE

A second word that describes the godly wife is *service.* Proverbs 31:13-21 describes a godly woman who lives a life of service to her family.

> She seeketh wool, and flax, and worketh willingly with her hands.
>
> She is like the merchants' ships; she bringeth her food from afar.
>
> She riseth also while it is yet night, and giveth meat to her household, and a portion to her maidens.
>
> She considereth a field, and buyeth it: with the fruit of her hands she planteth a vineyard.
>
> She girdeth her loins with strength, and strengtheneth her arms.
>
> She perceiveth that her merchandise is good: her candle goeth not out by night.
>
> She layeth her hands to the spindle, and her hands hold the distaff.
>
> She stretcheth out her hand to the poor; yea, she reacheth forth her hands to the needy.
>
> She is not afraid of the snow for her household: for all her household are clothed with scarlet.

And verse 27 adds, "She looketh well to the ways of her household, and eateth not the bread of idleness."

Here is a description of a woman whose life is spent in loving, faithful service. That is God's plan for all wives. Notice that the woman described here serves her husband, she serves her children, she serves the poor and needy, and she even serves her own servants. What a message about her love!

The woman that serves her family is following the example of the Lord Jesus, who came not to be ministered unto but to minister. There is no higher calling and privilege for the Christian wife and mother.

There are voices in our nation that call for the woman to assert herself. "Demand your rights," they say. "You have served and submitted long enough. Demand liberation from the chores of a housewife, and reach your full potential." The implication is that the woman who gives her life in service for her family is a second-class citizen, an underling who never quite makes it.

But I want you to notice that the woman described in Proverbs 31 is a woman who has reached the peak. Her service in the home has brought her a sense of personal fulfillment and the attainment of her highest potential. And her husband and children recognize it (Proverbs 31:28-29).

Women, service to your family is the highest calling to which you can rise. No career, no hobby, no occupation outside the home so fulfills God's purpose for a wife and mother. Are you a serving woman?

SACRIFICE

Closely related to service is a third word that describes the godly wife, and that is *sacrifice*. Real service demands sacrifice. The woman in Proverbs 31 sacrificed her sleep, her time, her money, and her strength to meet the needs of her family.

Every position in the family calls for submission, service, and sacrifice. But perhaps no position demands so much sacrifice as that of the wife and mother. From the painful experience of childbearing on, the life of a mother is one of sacrifice. There is not a mother worth her salt that does not know and cherish nights of sacrificed sleep with a sick and crying child. Mothers sacrifice their time, their strength, and sometimes even their own health to care for the needs of their children.

The wife and mother sacrifices to make the home attractive. She sacrifices to do the laundry, cook the food, care for the children, and care for her husband's personal needs.

Yes, the life of a Christian wife in a happy home is one of sacrifice. But it is a satisfying life. The woman who sacrifices knows exactly what the Lord meant when He urged us to lose our lives in order to find them. The loving sacrifice of a Christian mother and wife gives her life a depth and richness and meaningfulness that cannot be had in any other way.

And that is the idea of the fourth word that describes a godly wife.

SECURITY

Security. There is no sense of security quite like that of a woman whose husband and children rise up and call her blessed. She is secure in the knowledge that her husband loves her. She is secure in the knowledge that she perfectly fulfills God's will for her. She is secure in the love and fellowship of her home.

Have you known women like this? Surely you have. Their faces radiate with an inner glow. Wherever they go, they are a testimony to the wisdom of God's plan and pattern for the home. Their deep security can be sensed in everything about them. They know the spiritual security of a right

126

relationship with the Lord, and they know the emotional security of a right relationship with their husbands. They are truly glorious.

It is frightening to realize that our nation seems to be headed at a breakneck pace in totally the other direction. Women seem to be making a mass exodus from the home. One-third of our total work force is made up of women (well over 20 million). Many of those are mothers and wives who have left home for a career, seeking security and a sense of accomplishment in a job.

Listen to this shocking statement. Dr. Jeanne Binstock, professor of sociology at the University of Massachusetts, states that in twenty years, mothers will be "a mere specialty group in the United States"—like plumbers, auto workers, or engineers. "We . . . need to demand," says Dr. Binstock, "that the ancient occupation of motherhood fall into disrepute, and that women commit themselves to other occupations. Women must be liberated to enjoy the fruits of other occupations, whether they want to or not."

Surprised? You shouldn't be. That is just an echo of what many men and women have been screaming now for years. And more women take up the cry every day. Our nation is headed in a direction that is frightening. And the ones who will suffer most are the women. Real security can come only through obedience to God's plan and purpose. When motherhood falls into disrepute, as it already has in some circles, the possibility of genuine security and happiness for women will be destroyed.

Christian wife and mother, are you living the life of a godly wife? Are you submissive, serving, and sacrificing? And are you secure in your position? God wants you to be.

14

Husbands at the Helm

There is perhaps no failure as widespread and tragic as the failure of husbands and fathers. Ignorance, apathy, and rebellion against God's will have led to the abdication by many husbands of their authority and responsibilities. In millions of homes across our nation, the father is no more than a breadwinner, a live-in paycheck who, in some cases, merely supplements the income of the wife. He has no authority, and he wants none because he fears the responsibility that goes with it. He is content to devote his time to his career, letting his wife and children fend for themselves in regard to their spiritual and emotional needs.

In other homes the father is a domineering, demanding man who abuses his wife and children and sees their existence as being merely for the gratification of his desires. The ideas of sacrifice and service are totally foreign to him. He is self-centered, egotistical, and unconcerned about the needs of his family and his responsibility to them.

In our last message we examined some of the characteristics of a godly wife and mother. In this message we look at the responsibilities of the husband.

It is apparent from the state of families in our nation that something is dreadfully wrong. Families are falling apart, children are torn between parents in the tangled web of divorce, and problems like child abuse and battered wives are steadily on the increase. How much of those problems are the fathers' fault? Quite a bit.

129

It is my opinion that the responsibility for a godly, successful, happy home lies chiefly with the father. He has been designated by God as the one responsible for the leadership of the family, and so he is responsible for the way the family is led. No matter what influence may threaten the family, be it an influence from the inside or one from without, the father is the one responsible to deal with it and counteract it. Fathers, listen closely! If you would have godly, harmonious homes ordered after God's pattern, you must take the initiative. You must assume the leadership because it has been given to you by God.

The first thing, then, that you must understand is your position. You cannot assume the role God has established for the husband and father unless you know what it is. The Bible very clearly points out the responsibilities of each family member. The home was ordained by God. It was the first and most important unit of human government, and it is both the foundation and the building block out of which all other divine institutions are constructed.

And God gives explicit instructions about how it is to operate, not the least of which are the duties of each family member.

God's instructions to family members are found in Colossians 3:18-21. "Husbands," writes Paul in verse 19, "love your wives, and be not bitter against them." And that is the first of three characteristics of the godly husband and father I would like to examine today.

HE IS A LOVER

He is a lover. By that I do not mean what you may think I mean. He is romantic with his wife, to be sure, but he loves her with a sacrificial love that goes deeper than romantic love. When Paul wrote the same thing to the Ephesians, he added one idea: "even as Christ also loved the church, and gave himself for it" (Ephesians 5:25).

The love of a husband is to be a giving, sacrificial love, like the love of Christ for His church. And what did Christ give for the church? "Himself," Paul reminds us. The depth of Christ's love and sacrifice for the church cannot be sounded, and it is representative of the kind of love and sacrifice a husband is to have for his wife. Without that immeasurable, totally committed, giving kind of love, there is not the divine spark in marriage God intended it to have.

How is a husband to love his wife? If he truly loves his wife, he will be considerate and kind. He will be compassionate and tender and never hard or harsh. Love is not rough and tough, rude and crude; it is generous, courteous, and kind.

Look at the characteristics of godly love in 1 Corinthians 13:4-8:

> [Love] suffereth long, and is kind; [love] envieth not; [love] vaunteth not itself, is not puffed up,
>   Doth not behave itself unseemly, seeketh not her own, is not easily provoked, thinketh no evil;
>   Rejoiceth not in iniquity, but rejoiceth in the truth;
>   Beareth all things, believeth all things, hopeth all things, endureth all things.
> [Love] never faileth.

Is your love for your wife and family like that? Is it patient, kind, generous, self-depreciating, humble, well-behaved, serving, and pure?

What was the kind of love Christ showed for the church? Its real essence was the spirit of unselfishness. Jesus had existed in the form of God from eternity, but He did not consider that position something to be grasped for personal pleasure. He was willing to lay it aside to become a man and die even the lowest form of death for mankind (Philippians 2:5-8).

Husband, if your love for your wife and family is a

131

reflection of that kind of love, you probably are experiencing a happy home. Men, do you see this truth? We are not here for personal gratification. The family is a service organization, and our duties involve doing, not demanding; sacrificing, not being served; and giving, not getting. The family does not exist to serve the father; he exists to serve them.

Are you aware of your family's needs? Are you demonstrating a serving, sacrificial love as you seek to meet those needs?

HE IS A LEADER

A second characteristic of a godly husband is that *he is a leader.* Paul wrote to the wives in Ephesians 5:22, "Wives, submit yourselves unto your own husbands, as unto the Lord. For the husband is the head of the wife, even as Christ is the head of the church: and he is the saviour of the body." In those instructions to the wives, Paul conceals, almost subliminally, a message to the husbands. Along with the truth that the husband is the head is the emphasis of the truth that as head, he is responsible to nurture and protect. Christ is the head of the church, Paul says, *and the savior of the body.* And just as He used His position of leadership for the more important function of ministry, so a husband is to use his position as head of the household as an opportunity to be a servant.

Husband, what do you see when you look at your position? The authority? No—the responsibility. The greatest thing to understand about being head of your home is the truth that with that position comes an overwhelming responsibility.

You are responsible to provide for your family's needs—not just their material needs, but their emotional and spiritual needs as well. You are responsible to nurture your family, to protect them from any kind of harm. You are

132

responsible to teach your children, to train them in the way of righteousness and the Word of God. But most of all you are responsible to take the spiritual leadership.

Spiritual leadership in the family is a responsibility that probably more fathers abdicate than any other. Many a father, unsure or insecure in taking his place at the spiritual helm of the family, gives that responsibility to the wife or just neglects it altogether.

Perhaps this is at the heart of all paternal failure. It is the one area that is more easily attacked than any other, because it involves the most time, labor, and concern. But it also is one of the least externally visible of all parental duties.

Father, if you are going to fulfill your role as the spiritual leader of your family, it will involve a tremendous sacrifice in terms of time spent alone with the Lord in His Word and in prayer. Your private devotional life is vital to your family's spiritual well-being. Your personal walk with the Lord is more important to your family than anyone else's, because God uses you, as the spiritual leader, to deal with your family.

Spiritually, it is often true that as the father goes, so goes the family. Joshua spoke for his family. "As for me and my house," he said, "we will serve the Lord" (Joshua 24:15). The Philippian jailer's whole family believed and was saved because of his faith (Acts 16:34).

On the other hand, think of the many fathers in the Bible who saw their families corrupted or destroyed because of carelessness in their spiritual lives. Noah, Lot, Eli, and David all are examples of men who failed in their personal spiritual lives and saw their families bear the fruit of their failure.

It is sobering to realize that our responsibility to our families is of that magnitude. Certainly the job of being head of a home is not easy! The extent of our responsibility is awesome.

But our responsibility goes far beyond our personal spiritual lives and extends to the lives of the individuals in our family as well. One of the requirements for an elder in the church is that he have "faithful children not accused of riot or unruly" (Titus 1:6). "Faithful" in that verse means "believing," and it places the responsibility for the spiritual condition of the child squarely on the shoulders of the father.

Fathers, you are responsible for the spiritual health of the individuals in your family. That is part of your responsibility as a leader. And yet most fathers do not even know very much about the personal spiritual lives of their children. If you are going to fulfill your complete responsibility to your family, you are going to have to be able to communicate effectively with them about spiritual matters. That will involve spending time with them — quality time, discussing the things of the Lord.

Yes, leadership is an awesome responsibility. It is not something that happens on its own. It involves hard work. And that brings to mind the third characteristic of a godly husband.

HE IS A LABORER

The truly godly husband is a *laborer*. There is no room for sloth in the business of fatherhood. Paul wrote to Timothy, "If any provide not for his own, and especially for those of his own house, he hath denied the faith, and is worse than an infidel" (1 Timothy 5:8).

There is no question that Paul was speaking primarily of the material provision a father should provide for his family, but the father's provision for the family goes much further than that, as we have seen. A father must labor to supply every need of his family, and again, that involves a great sacrifice.

Are you beginning to get the idea? The father's duties are

all sacrificial. He does them asking nothing in return. He gives and yields, and sacrifices, and then he does it some more.

The father is a laborer. He is a laborer *for* his family. But he is a laborer *in* his family as well. The father works to assure that there is harmony in the home. His is not an easy job. All that he does must be done with wisdom and fairness and understanding.

And he also is a laborer with his family. Their goals are his goals. He provides encouragement, incentive, and correction when needed. He prays with the family, worships with the family, and studies with the family. He must be sympathetic, patient, reasonable, and diplomatic. He must see clearly where the family is going and be able to give direction.

And above all, he must understand that he is a laborer *among* his family. The Christian father must be an example. He must represent what he expects his children to become.

I heard of a father who returned home from work to hear his small son and daughter quarreling, yelling, and threatening one another. It appeared that they were about to come to blows.

"What's wrong with you kids?" he demanded.

Frowns turned to smiles. The little boy tilted his chin and said, "Nothing. We were just playing Papa and Mama."

I hope that father hung his head in shame. We must realize just how influential our lives are on our children. They see us more clearly than anyone out in the world. And it is imperative that we give them a good example.

That is the way it should be in the Christian home. Daily Bible reading and prayer should be as regular as meals. The father should be the head of the house—a lover, a leader, and a laborer.

May your home be built on the solid and unchanging standard of God's precious Word.